Friends, Partners, & Lovers

Marks of a Vital Marriage

D0168380

Friends, Partners, & Lovers

Marks of a Vital Marriage

Warren Lane Molton

JUDSON PRESS ® VALLEY FORGE

Friends, Partners, & Lovers: Marks of a Vital Marriage,
Revised Edition
©1993
Judson Press, Valley Forge, PA 19482-0851

Library of Congress Cataloging-in-Publication Data

Molton, Warren Lane.
  Friends, partners and lovers: marks of a vital marriage / by Warren Lane Molton. – Rev. ed.
    p. cm.
    Includes bibliographical references and index
    ISBN 0-8170-1187-0
    1. Marriage. 2. Interpersonal relations. 3. Self-actualization
(Psychology) I. Title.
HQ734.M79 1993
646.7'8 – dc20   93-16196

Printed in the U.S.A.   Cover design by Ife Designs + Associates

      94 95 96 97 98 99 00 01   9 8 7 6 5 4 3 2

For Dian

Friend, Partner, and Lover

CONTENTS

PREFACE

In reading the new edition of *Friends, Partners, and Lovers*, I find my reflections gathering around two particular areas of thought. The first has to do with my professional work as a Jungian psychotherapist, a career for which I had only just begun to prepare when the book was first published in 1979. The second area of thought about the book is of a more personal nature, perhaps because I realize how much our own lives have been shaped by that material and the processes of constructive confrontation that it suggests. For most of our adult lives, Warren and I have been grappling with ideas about marriage that keep moving us along on both our separate paths of development and our life together. So I would like to reflect briefly, from a personal standpoint, on how some of these ideas have affected me.

As a practicing psychotherapist, I find the fundamental tenets of this book to be enormously useful. The second edition embraces important new material while maintaining the basic vocabulary and approach of the first. Concepts such as covenant and contract and the three categories of relationship expressed in the title are in almost daily use for me in my work.

And the new material on love, work, and play comes at a time when most of us feel the need to reevaluate our priorities in these areas of life. Also, I like the way Warren uses acrostics as a means of developing the metaphoric language that deepens our understanding of an idea such as work or play. This is in itself a sort of creative play with the unconscious world in which language is an imaginal art form. So I have come to appreciate the book very much in these ways.

In a more personal vein, I am aware, of course, that the tasks to which I apply my conscious effort regarding living in relationship with Warren have changed dramatically as our family and careers have matured. I'm not sure just when I stopped being defensive about what I felt my shortcomings were in either domain and started feeling more playful and relaxed about it all. Perhaps it was when Warren began thinking and writing about considering play not as a reward for good work but as an essential component of creative living. Or perhaps it happened when I realized that my own path of growth and development, which required that I live some of the time in a psychological and spiritual world entirely unto myself, as an *opposite* of but not a *contradiction* to relational living. The tension between those two polarities has become dynamic and energizing rather than exhausting and riddled with guilt and doubt. *Friends, Partners, and Lovers* has taught me much about the management of that creative tension and how to negotiate what I need.

I still believe that there is a way for human beings to live in long-term relationships in both freedom and union. That belief has not wavered in these fourteen years. I believe, also, that I know a little bit more about how to do it than I did then. There are new ideas here. We are still learning. And it is still really worth doing.

Mary Dian Molton

INTRODUCTION

It is with deep gratitude that I thank the readers who so enjoyed and recommended *Friends, Partners and Lovers* that after ten years of reprintings, a new edition now seems called for.

Both lay and professional readers have offered suggestions regarding the book, causing me to review every word of the original text, adding new ideas and illustrations where they seemed appropriate. Many felt the book was too brief, so it has been expanded and, I hope enriched with the development of additional chapters on the ABC's of communication, sexuality, and my attempt to integrate the celebrative arenas of love, work, and play. The bibliography has also been expanded for those who want to explore the general territory of the book.

Again, I thank those of you who wrote or spoke with me at workshops, conferences, and therapy sessions, as well as family and close friends who have been especially supportive of my work as both therapist and writer. I want to express my deep thanks to a few who have been especially close to me in the preparation of this book. These include our grown children, Stephen, Jennifer, and David, and grandsons, Eric and Aaron, who take our family into the next generation; our dear family friend, Helga Beuing, who has unstintingly and devotedly assisted with the preparation of this new manuscript like a midwife; my friend, Paul Jones, whose friendship and probing dialogue with me is valued beyond measure; to long-time friends and colleagues, Karen Woods, Mary Welsh, Larry Nieters, Sharon Cohen, Joyce Davidson, Marti Rees, Barbara Beckerman, Donna Pendergrass, and Jean Erwin of my staff; to our daughter, Jennifer, for her special talents given generously for this book and the Center; to my special friends, John Morrison and Jeff Fryer, lay leaders in my therapy groups, where many aspects of my books have been tested; to my friend, Jack Taylor, a one-man cheering section and distribution center for both books; to Harris Parker, friend of longest standing, for inviting me to Columbia College to share ideas of this book for a week with faculty and student body; and to a couple of young buddies who have become excellent therapists over the years of our talking and sharing and who have given me so much, Steve Walker and Andy Vos; to good friends Sally and Mike Shaffer for their inspiration; to my dear brother- and sister-in-law, Ellis and Marcie, who just stay there like stars; and finally to Dian once more, whose love continues to be for me one of the truly great realities of my life. To all of those and so many others as friends and clients, and clients who became friends, I offer my profound appreciation and invite you to call or write and share.

Warren Lane Molton
Kansas City, Missouri

Chapter 1

AUTONOMY: KEY TO THE ADULT PERSON

The most crucial element in the creation of a healthy marriage is the healthy adult, and the truly healthy adult is autonomous. To be autonomous is to be in charge of one's own life, to be able to say, "I belong to me. I accept responsibility for me. I command my life and sit in the driver's seat. I am not on my knees in the back looking out the window at what someone else has driven me through. Nor am I even in the passenger's seat up front sharing the decisions and viewing firsthand where I am going. I am, rather, behind the wheel, keeping my life on the road, and moving toward my destination. If I do not belong to me, I belong to someone else."

I may commit myself to another person, some great cause, a personal task, or a religion. Still, I must begin by owning me. Since I cannot give what I do not own, I must first establish ownership of myself, taking charge of my life. Then I may freely give myself to a relationship transcending me.

Some of us may still belong to our parents, even though we call ourselves adults. They own us, setting out goals, making decisions, and offering unsolicited criticism. They may use their own hurt feelings, anger, money, ill humor, ridicule, or rejection to maintain control over us. They may even rule us from the grave. Knuckling under to what Eric Berne called "critical parent" tapes may keep us childish, enslaved, and can prevent us from becoming autonomous adults.

Once, in an effort to illustrate for me his father's fits of temper, a client described how that rage-filled parent – drunk and insulted when my client refused to obey an order to do an errand that could wait – came over on his tractor and plowed up his son's front yard, even as the grandchildren watched in disbelief. Disobeying his father was often to court disaster, and breaking the critical parent tapes was an awful task.

Even religion can direct our lives without becoming an integral part of our own belief system. It can be a mechanical process by which we simply obey religious laws, rituals, and expectations in the community. We may uncritically carry out religious orders like obedient children; or we may agree that certain religious behavior is required, and so we ritually obey. Religion ought to have personal meaning, a meaning that you and I understand and cherish. It is not enough that it is meaningful for my parents, or that my mate needs and wants it, or that I should be a good example to my children. Religion is my personal attempt to understand the meaning of my life. The idea of religion as the "friendly cop" is repulsive. Nor is religion the "handbook" or "multiplication table" by which I transact my purchase of life. It is not my governor, keeper, or jailer. Rather, my religion is like a friend, whom I love, and with whom I attempt to understand and *do* life. I can embrace this friend. I may also challenge and debate my friend. We may even have to part company, briefly or forever. My friend does not own me.

Some of us *belong* to a vocational group, a business organization, a club, or a neighborhood. The control of goals and patterns is relinquished to the *other*, so that we are held captive by that group and dare not make a move at odds with the group. A man once told me: "We have a block party every Labor Day, and you decide to do something other than go to that party, and I'll swear they'd egg your house. Your own neighbors!"

We can be under the rule of spouse or children. We defer to them and feel manipulated. Any sense of "I belong to me" is lost. There is no time for privacy. A woman locks herself in her bathroom every morning for half an hour to "escape my two- and three-year-olds." A man angrily said to me, "We didn't have our children. They had us. To take care of them. To give, give, give. Well, I've had it. I've been *had* enough." If our spouse or children own us, it is our fault. We let it happen. We may even have asked for it, until it got out of hand. There are many ways to be owned, all of which deny autonomy.

The situation may develop quite innocently. In one instance, a divorced woman married a second time and her new husband moved in with her. The mortgage was held by her father, who had helped her keep the house for the sake of her twin sons. Father had a say in everything regarding the property. Eventually the new husband resented the house, her father, and his wife. His feelings of being an equal partner were destroyed. Father refused to sell the house to the couple for fear that the new husband might also leave his daughter and get an unfair share of the property, including father's investment. The husband was not autonomous in that arrangement and felt owned by his father-in-law. Another divorce, the very thing this parent most feared, was coming to pass because of his paranoia about his daughter's husband. The young husband's feeling of being trapped and controlled brought them into counseling. His sense of helplessness soon turned to rage at the father-in-law, leading to a major confrontation with him, and a settlement that restored ownership to the couple. The marriage suffered great stress during this process.

A *negative* check for autonomy is the "Who is to blame?" question. The blaming person does not feel in charge. Problems are not solved but are transferred to someone else or to circumstances. If we, in the face of a setback, accuse someone else for the situation we have not yet taken in hand, we are looking for a scapegoat. The blaming person needs an excuse, an out, for not assuming responsibility. "How can you expect me to be autonomous," a client asks, "with controlling parents like mine?" That man was a forty-three-year-old banker.

A *positive* check for autonomy has to do with taking an inventory of our own resources. How do I handle being alone? Can I meet normal financial obligations? Do I get problems solved? Am I an action person? Do I take care of my body? Am I aware of my emotional needs and how to get them met without exploiting someone else or getting "ripped off"? Do I live creatively in my environment without exhausting myself or the gifts of that environment? Or do I say, "If only I had been born rich, or beautiful, or talented, or into a great family"? Being in charge of my own life means to know and understand the universe of me and how I can best command my destiny with the resources available to me. I do not complain about what has been done to me. Life is not an "If only . . ." but a "What if . . . ." Risk is the key.

Adults are those who have achieved significant autonomy, are their own caretakers, and believe that success or failure is essentially in their own hands. There is always the possibility of personal disaster resulting from circumstances beyond our control, but the goal of the self is to remain in charge. It is hard to imagine a price too high to pay in order to maintain *autonomy: personal freedom with responsibility among one's peers.*

One of the tragedies of our culture is that most of our systems foster dependency. Any time we create cookie cutter lookalikes, we reduce personal and individual initiative, energy, and imagination. We are then teaching people to function as parts of a gigantic machine, or sheep in theological systems, or apprentices to stereotyped professions, or voters in dehumanizing political power blocks. We destroy the individual's right to discover his or her own life. It is not strange, then, that not too long ago some of our brightest and most creative young people turned to the soil, using simple methods and tools to create life-supporting farms, giving enormous time and energy to the simple tasks of growing and harvesting, nurturing and protecting. Even now, a brief news clip from an annual Future Farmers Association convention offers the same sort of refrain when young people attending were asked if they would stay on the farm. Their replies speak of freedom, independence, autonomy, and even: "to take care of the land!" This Garden, this Eden!

These young people did not have an answer to our ills, but they at least offered alternatives to the dependency syndrome. Among the most cherished and established professions of medicine, law, education, and the ministry, the quest for autonomy has created mavericks who open free clinics, are legal counselors for the poor and disfranchised, and start alternative schools and churches in homes. They are responding to a need to feel empowered and to give individuals the feeling of being in charge of their own destiny. An old woman, who might have lived longer than she did, refused to go to a hospital because, she said, "They take over more than's theirs."

Autonomy may suggest to some that marriage is obsolete. They might assume that the autonomous person cannot enter into any relationship that diminishes personal autonomy. To say this is to miss the point. Autonomy does not foreclose relational contracts. Rather, the individual is better equipped to enter the relationship freely and creatively. He or she now can be an adult, with a power field to commit to another strong, autonomous person. Together they effect an alliance of strength and resources that can facilitate private and corporate goals. They invite, encourage, and enable one another. Their common good is bound up in the realization of each other's potential. They are free to negotiate from self-knowledge and are then able to relinquish and exchange gifts without reserve or defensiveness.

Perspective: Inner-Directed

The perspective, or life-view, of the autonomous adult is that of the inner-directed person, suggested by David Riesman in *The Lonely Crowd*, and is contrasted with the outer- and other-directed person.

The inner-directed adult views life from this side of things. The outlook is from inside out, one which says, "I view life from my own door, and I seek my way in terms of my own basic needs, with an enlightened concern for others. To face life realistically, I must be able to view it out of my history, and from my spot in the world." It was with these feelings that a young man declined his father's offered gift of the lot next door on which to build his home, and said, "My father's world and mine are very different, and walking out on the same street to pick up the same paper every morning won't fix things as he would hope."

If I am outer-directed, I determine my way according to what others want of me. By seeking out their desires, I am distracted from me and may very well lose touch with myself, ignore my talents, and miss my own destiny. A premedical student was the third child of a family in which her mother, father, and older brothers were all physicians. She was also engaged to a medical student. During college, she had enjoyed acting and wanted to pursue a master's degree in theater. Her fiancé was sympathetic but disappointed, and her own family ridiculed the whole idea. Her parents finally said that they would not finance such a program. After college graduation, she became depressed, broke her engagement, and took a nonlethal overdose of drugs. Her suicidal gesture was a protest against the helpless feeling of being controlled by the expectations of others. Clearly, she was not ready for marriage.

After a little more than three months of therapy, she liked herself better, told her parents she was never going into medicine, concluded her relationship with her fiancé, found a job and an apartment, and enrolled in the theater department of the local state university. She laughed one day and said, "Even my voice is stronger." Everything about her, even the way she walked, communicated strength and commitment. Today, some years later, she is a surer and happier person. Her perspective moved from outside to inside. This is the perspective of Jung's concept of individuation—becoming, as an acorn becomes an oak—what you were intended to be, your true self.

The other-directed person is ruled by concepts of transcendence, such as the will of God. The *other* may also be some special cause by which one's will is captured and ruled.

I have counseled seminary students who believed they were called into ministry at a very early age, even as young as five years old. They believed the decision was closed and should never be challenged. Occasionally, such single-minded commitment ignores serious deficits and may in fact even be confirmed as God's will by those very deficits, as with one student who stuttered. He said to me, "Moses probably stuttered. If God would call a stutterer, he must surely want him badly, and have something special for him to do. How can I not obey?" This man did nothing about correcting the stutter, refusing to enter therapy after his wife had brought him to a counselor. He was really not free to examine his life from any point if it challenged "God's call." It was a major defense system for him, and he was not going to venture out long enough to find out what freedom is about. At age eleven he had been "called" to the ministry. It was an obsession that preempted discussion of most of the critical life decisions and made him unavailable for serious debate regarding his wife's needs, where the children would be reared, salary problems, and other subjects that threatened an absolute allegiance to the simple notion of "God's got me, and nothing else matters." How much better if he had been able to own himself and create relationships with a gift of himself. Instead, an overriding, absolute, blind obedience to one experience at age eleven determined all his relationships and left him in what he called his "happy prison." If his rage ever emerges, it will be an ugly thing to see. Now he has it contained in his "God box."

This man might be dismissed as a religious fanatic and not typical of commitment to some transcending person or cause. However, hardly a month passes that I do not see or hear of someone who has a similar obsession in other professions. Medicine occasionally has its own special sort of physician or nurse given to such messianic visions. Every cause has its saviors.

The perspective of the autonomous adult is that of one who is inner-directed. To be such a person, or to be in the process of becoming such a person, means working at creating a person of unity and coherence. The elements of my ego bind together in an integrated whole, and I function inside and outside as one who is in fact, as we say, together.

Unity

Autonomy greatly depends upon my understanding of myself as a thinking, feeling, acting, and believing person. A helpful construct looks like this:

Thinking: Reasoning, comprehending, judging and remembering with goal-centered ideas, symbols, metaphors, and associations, stimulated by a need or task, and leading toward a realistic solution

Believing: Values, philosophy or theology that provides an understanding of the meaning of one's life— the spiritual dimension

Feeling: The color of life, including all the hues, tones, tints, and intensity of our full emotional spectrum.

Acting: The energy or movement, doing and causing things to occur for change, growth, and development

I THINK

anger   apathy

I FEEL   anxiety   I ACT

Self Sphere

I understand me as I see how I function in each of these areas. It may seem that my thinking and feeling decide my action. This is not always true, however, as it may be only when I act that I begin to know my real feelings or thoughts. Recently I asked a man how his wife's anger made him feel. Sitting next to her on the love seat, he said he did not know. With that she flung her hand out and bopped him on his shoulder. Needless to say, his feelings were quickly triggered. Her action tripped his feelings. This process is clear.

It is sometimes harder if our feelings are more deeply buried. It may be only by acting that these feelings thaw out and begin to emerge. It is like not knowing how you feel about cauliflower until you taste it. Often, to shake hands or touch someone's arm clarifies feelings. To begin talking may bring tears or a relaxing laughter. Certain actions stimulate feelings and are like priming the feeling pump. It still amazes me when a couple with frosty feelings and merely polite communication, are willing to hold hands and gaze quietly at one another for a few moments and are able then to unleash a flood of feelings. The touch of hand and eye opens the way.

Therefore, the triangle works in any direction, and it may start from any one of the three corners. Problems most often emerge when one corner of the triangle is in conflict with the other two. For example: Cover the *thinking* corner with your thumb. You are now working off the *feeling-acting* axis (if it feels good, do it). This sounds like fun; but if the thinking process is blocked, you may be in trouble. A man was enjoying an affair until he suddenly thought: "This is exactly what my father was doing before Mother was killed in the auto wreck." The *feeling-acting* system threw him into great anxiety. He became impotent, could not sleep, and lost considerable weight. His question was, "Why did it take two months for my head to plug into that situation?" A memory of his father triggered his own thought processes, which helped him reflect upon his *feeling-acting* trap.

The relevance of the triangle can be further seen by covering either of the other two corners. If you cover *feeling*, you work off the *thinking-acting* axis. Persons who block emotion in this way often seem wooden and automatic. You never know their feelings. They keep feelings covered and may have rather bland personalities. If we block feelings, we may get into a rut. We become *routinized*. Life gets dull. We are trapped in a ritual. An unhappy wife said, "I simply thought, 'you are married, now act married.' I did that for six years, and I have lost all my feelings for my husband. I buried them and one day I realized that they were gone." And with a bitter smile she concluded, "I guess my feelings just rotted." The result of blocking feelings is *apathy*, an indifferent, "who cares?" attitude. To know and accept feelings is to open up the triangle and permit new action based on feeling demands. Her divorce might have come sooner and her marriage might have ended rather than simply rotting. However, her marriage might also have been saved if she had honored her feelings and addressed her spouse with them.

Now cover the *acting* corner. You say to your spouse, "I have a great idea that I am really excited about." You describe it and are then informed that your mate has no intention of doing such a thing, no matter how you feel about it. Action is blocked and the result is apt to be frustration and anger. The triangle wants to flow. We begin to hurt when one corner is blocked. If two are blocked or diminished, it registers in the personality with varying consequences, usually with enormous stress that leaves the person immobilized. Healthy action is the most convincing message to the ego. Wants and needs are the goals of the triangle. "I want to make love because my *thinking* and *feeling* tell me that this is a pleasurable act that is congruent with my *beliefs* about the relationship."

Still, the *believing* at the Center is the key to the healthy functioning of the adult person. This has to do with my values, priorities, commitments, and my own personal life vision — what Carl Jung called "one's own private myth." These make up the great integrating force of my life, bind me together, and directly influence what I think, feel, and do. It is at this Center that I discover and declare the *meaning* of my life and perhaps in a philosophical or theological system set out my understanding of what that is.

The Center directs, instructs, and equips the business of the other three areas. The Center carries the characteristics of an informing wisdom. It is not just a cop or jailer. The Center is more the honored maestro conducting the symphonic movements of the personality as a harmony of thought, feeling, and

action mobilize the person to do life with creativity and satisfaction. In marriage we are constantly seeking stimulation and
compatibility in all of these areas. There must be enough congruence between husband and wife regarding life meaning,
thinking process, feeling systems, and action to permit a fulfilling exchange.

On our thirtieth wedding anniversary, Dian and I spent the
afternoon reflecting on our years together, as we enjoyed a pic-
nic on a mountain overlooking Aspen, Colorado. It was a beautiful day in August, and we shared why we believed we were still
together when so many of our friends were divorced. There were
lots of good reasons, but the most important seemed to be that
we shared the same values. These values were not so much a
moral or religious set, some theological system. We simply
cared deeply about the same things. These were the things in
which we invested our thinking, feeling, action, time, money,
and prayers – the great energies of our lives.

A young couple, briefly married, found that the husband's
new infatuation with bow-and-arrow hunting was creating problems. The wife saw it as a cruel sport that was quite unacceptable within her set of values. She resented everything about the
sport, felt weepy on the days he hunted and angry when he
came home, whether or not he had game. Quarrels resulted from
this situation. It appeared to be an isolated problem, that is,
not symptomatic of deeper problems. The wife discounted any
other inquiry about her jealousy, stubbornness, and insinua-
tions that seemed to attach to her concern over hunting. She re-
torted with statements, such as "Even a gun would not be quite
so bad." She insisted that all killing is evil, but the arrow, as a
"primitive and inaccurate" weapon, was torturous and obscene.
It became clear that the marriage would not abide bow-and-
arrow hunting. For the wife it was a value-ridden behavior, and,
in order to preserve the tranquillity of the marriage, the husband finally decided to discontinue the sport. The relationship
was immediately stabilized. He was disappointed but not spite-
ful, and his wife was obviously relieved and grateful. She had no
fear of his being vindictive, and he exhibited no sign of feeling
henpecked.

We all can cite similar examples of marital disharmony over
drugs, alcohol, infidelity, gambling, or other behavior that may

be unacceptable to a spouse. Many values are steadfast and are definitive aspects of persons. Clashes over values between mates may forecast disaster. Not all values can be checked out before marriage. Values change throughout marriage and should be newly contracted as they appear or evolve.

The belief system at the Center monitors and conditions. Inversely, it is also influenced by the other three systems – thinking, feeling, acting. Logic said to a young husband, whose wife was completely paralyzed after a skiing accident, that he should accept her suggestion that they divorce. However, the commitment at the Center, in dialogue with his reasoning processes, overrode his logic. He insisted that he loved her and would continue to be her husband. Such a decision affected the feelings that moved between them, and prescribed much of the action of the relationship. It conditioned plans for children, friendships, and their sex life. In fact, the entire relationship was profoundly changed by his decision to accept the impact of the accident and remain in the marriage. Another set of values, just as valid, might have caused a husband to accept his wife's offer, resulting in divorce and a chance to create a new marriage.

A belief system may not confront the thinking or even the feeling systems, permitting them to function freely, yet totally blocking an action that would seem to be the obvious outcome of certain thoughts and feelings. For example, an attractive young woman had erotic fantasies about a man in her office. Reflecting on this triangle, she was able to make sense of her ambivalence about acting on her feelings. She honestly said, "I like him a lot, I'm sexually aroused by him, and he is my male ideal. But he is happily married, so far as I can tell, and I will not take or allow action that might threaten that marriage. It is a matter of values. To consider an affair with him is selfish, destructive thinking which I reject, else I have trouble knowing who I am at the Center, where I locate conscience and personal dignity." Her value system demanded considerable discipline.

In terms of our triangle, blocked action should result in anger and frustration. However, this autonomous person, getting instructions from *within*, will not experience a disabling anger, and she can find acceptable ways to avoid or discharge the energies of frustration. There are available to her the traditional sublimations, alternative relationships, and perhaps even a discussion of her feelings with the man in question if that seems appropriate. While not creating high drama or ripe gossip with such a decision, such action is taken by people every day, even though it may mean denying themselves the pleasure of genuine love feelings. Some restructure their interactions and have been known to quit their jobs. Such governance from the Center is vital and necessary. Otherwise, we are at the mercy of our feelings and rationalizations, which may be insubstantial and unworthy.

It is important that the Center remain resilient and dynamic. These four systems are interlocking and dialogical, each having its own function, informing one another, and responding honestly to messages that circulate among them. It will be true that the soul quality of the Center that integrates and sets precedents will be influenced by what goes on in the other three systems.

Reports from the air crash victims who cannibalized the dead bodies of their comrades in order to survive clearly indicate that their action was a radical affront to their feelings and values, but reason told them the action was necessary to allow more time for the possibility of rescue. Their action was a temporary abridgment of their values; the human family must periodically examine such values if only for the sake of others who might find themselves in a similar tragic dilemma.

Occasionally in human history, extremity invents action resulting in new norms that set new behavioral patterns, especially in the field of medicine where the need for information may fly in the face of belief systems. This is illustrated in the simple process of medical postmortems. What was thought of as "butchering the image of God" gave way to the more acceptable notion of autopsy. While the *imago dei* might be offended by the scalpel, the need for information to benefit the living took precedence over the values in a theological system.

More personally, this same sort of thing may occur at the Center when one eats certain foods, takes a drink, adopts birth control, is thrown in with a member of a minority group, loses his or her virginity – all perhaps on a whim, or by accident, or as a desperate measure – and discovers new truth which creates a new value at the Center, which in turn affects the related thoughts, feelings, and action.

It is not possible to process the data of these four systems with their complex interactions and to measure their influence upon one another. Still, by reliable hunch, some subjective testimony, and a few "scientific observations" we know that there are many whole autonomous persons who grow, change, and expand as persons in a world of both menace and promise.

Once, while fishing in Connecticut, I saw a boy of about fourteen line cast a small fish he had caught toward a flock of gulls that hovered about his boat. A gull took the bait and immediately found itself tethered to a fishing line from which all the bird's hysterical wheeling and driving could not free it. The scene looked normal. The gull was still feeding off its environment, diving into familiar water, and climbing the air of its home. Yet everything was different. The bird was hooked, helplessly controlled by a person at the other end of a strong line. The young man played out the terrified gull, gradually subduing it, until it fell exhausted into Long Island Sound.

This is a fit analogy for what happens to many of us who refuse to take charge of our lives. The innocent gull was trapped by its ignorance and hunger, the prey of a pitiless youngster. All of the components do not fit, but the association of our life with this story is painfully clear: someone hooks us and tethers us to his or her will. Our only advantage over the poor gull is that we have more power to cut the cord. Or do we? That answer makes all the difference.

Chapter 2

SIX MODELS OF MARRIAGE

There are many ways to put marriage together, all of which may work to one degree or another. Many are distortions of what creative marriage can be, and they may be crippling to all who are connected with them, adults and children alike. In this chapter we consider some of the possibilities. There are countless others and combinations of these. It would seem helpful to get a clear image of how we do relationships. What needs are met? Are we loved or unloved, cared about, cherished, and celebrated, or lonely and in pain?

Doormat

The motto of the *doormat* marriage is "Me top dog, you underdog." Even the ring of it suggests a sadomasochistic alliance in which power, dominance, control, and perhaps terror are descriptive of the marriage, with one partner playing boss. Needless to say, this is a pathetic contract. These two are not equal. One is inferior, accepts a dehumanizing treatment, and surrenders autonomy. The other is a tyrant.

Couples who live this way remind me of Hank and Alice who

had married at age seventeen when Alice was three months pregnant. They were thirty-nine when I first met Alice, who had spent twenty years in misery, except for the fourteen months when Hank served in Korea. Alice came to see me alone, after a fight in which Hank had left her face badly bruised and her upper lip split. She was, under normal conditions, an attractive woman. Although fifteen or twenty pounds overweight, she was clearly aware of her hair and clothes, and gave them care and attention. Her blue eyes seemed sad. Her voice was husky from too many cigarettes. She reported that she had gone to family service counseling at least four times over the years for one session each time, but treatment was discouraged unless her husband agreed to accompany her.

After the fight, Alice had fled to Hank's sister's house three blocks away from their house, and the sister refused to take her in for the night unless she agreed to see me. She doubted that Hank would come. He had refused before. She told me that I should not telephone him. "It would only make him mad," she said. She wondered if there were something *she* could do.

"You could threaten to leave him unless he agrees to get help," I suggested.

She responded, "Oh, I could never do that. He'd kill me. That's clear. I tried to leave twelve years ago, and he came out the door after me with his rifle. Besides, the kids need their father." There were three boys: the oldest was away in the navy and other two were sixteen and seventeen years old.

"Is there anything good about living with Hank?" I asked.

"Oh my, yes! I work and have my own car. He would never hear of such a thing just three years ago. We have a nicer home than either of my sisters. And just last Christmas Hank gave me a new sewing machine. He has his good points."

"What do you two do together?" I asked.

"What do you mean?" She frowned. "You mean, like sex?"

"Well, I was really thinking of activities, parties, getting out. Recreation, things like that."

"Oh, we do lots of things together. Mostly in the summer, though. Hank likes to fish, and two years ago we got a speedboat so we could water ski, but we didn't do much of that last summer. Hank fell down the basement stairs and twisted his back." There was a pause. She stared at me, then out the window. "And as far as sex is concerned, it's okay. I never got much out of it. Hank was always too fast for me." She darted a glance at me. "You know, he comes quick."

"Did you talk about this with Hank?"

"Heavens no! I'm not that crazy. I remember once he came home and said one of the men at work told him that his wife moaned a lot when she came, and he wondered why I didn't, and I said, 'Because it doesn't *hurt*.' And Hank just laughed and laughed at that. We never mentioned it again. That must have been seven, eight years ago."

"How is it now?"

"You mean sex?" I nodded. "Tell the truth, we don't do it much any more. After his beer every night, he pretty much falls asleep, and that's it. I'm usually so tired it's just as well. Of course now and then after company or something special with our friends – a couple across the street – he'll come after me and we do it, but it doesn't take any time at all. So I don't mind occasionally."

I asked if she were satisfied with this arrangement, and raising her brows she answered, "Yeah, I guess."

I offered to see her again and she said, "What can you do for me if Hank won't come? He's funny. He might even come after you if I told him you wanted to see him." There was the slightest smile.

"What will you do?" I asked.

"Same as always, I guess. Make the best of it. What can I do? Leave? He'd find me."

"The police could help."

"How? He knows all the tricks. He'd have them eating out of his hand. He was an MP in the army. Besides, he's pretty mean sometimes. I believe he really could kill me. He knocked out our boy Tom with his bare fist once. Hit him right in the jaw."

"How about your families?"

She laughed. "They're as scared of him as I am. Besides, his father is dead. My daddy told me once when I went over there after a fight that I probably deserved it if I talked to Hank the way I used to talk to him and Mama. That was fifteen years ago. He never did anything to help. Hank's mother is in a rest home." She smiled. "There's nobody really, Doctor."

I suggested that their marriage may be a destructive game

between them, as though Hank had some need to hurt her and she to suffer. To this she replied, "Oh, that's not true at all. I hope you don't think I enjoy all of this." She ran her hand across her face, lightly touching her lips.

Then I said, "All I know is that this has been going on for twenty years and everyone in your world seems helpless to stop it, and you refuse to leave him in order to give credibility to your complaints. I understand the risk in taking action against Hank, even in your coming here, but staying there is perhaps even more risky. And certainly nothing will change as things now stand. I would like to suggest that you begin to sort all of this out, and put together a plan of action that could be helpful for both of you. You do have other options."

She smiled, stood to leave, thanked me, and said, "It's no use, Doctor."

I wished her well, and suggested that she return if she wanted to. "Don't worry about me. I'll be just fine. I'm used to all this by now." She chatted briefly with my receptionist, paid the fee and left. I never saw her again.

In their "doormat marriage," Alice and Hank lived in a complex system of signals, messages, hostile acts, and mock defense gestures by which they accomplished their ends. Hank hated and Alice hurt. Yet there were the goodies: house, sewing machine, her own car and job, and the fishing and water skiing. The fights seemed to be Hank's answer to his deep feelings of inadequacy, anxiety over sexual function, and hostility toward women. Alice clearly felt a need to be punished because of her guilt feelings growing out of her relationship to her parents. This is only a descriptive explanation. The day-to-day problem was that the major arenas of marriage were in shambles. They had no concept of what it meant to be friends. They were not partners: Hank "permitted" her to have certain privileges. Their love was like a battered child. Their fights were a substitute for emptiness: something was better than nothing. Even bad feelings were better than no feelings at all. A man once said to me, "Yeah, we'd rather fight than have sex. More exciting."

Yet contrary to popular misconceptions, this might not have been an impossible situation. The marriage might have become much more healthy and rewarding for both of them had they been willing to work at it. Alice was not able to act, perhaps out of the *habit* of the marriage and her need to be punished. Hank may have sensed this, and getting her double message ("Let's get help"/"No, I'm not serious"), he was not compelled to examine the relationship. Alice was not convincing. It would have taken a bold act on her part, something with clout, to get Hank's attention.

There were a number of alternatives. There could have been help from the police and the courts, especially after the evidence of their bitter fights. But Alice was not willing to press charges and move persuasively for help. Only a tragedy might have brought them to a counselor, such as a very serious problem with a son and a court order for psychiatric help.

As a counselor, I am still surprised to find how many young couples report having come from homes in which their parents regularly engaged in acrimony and/or fights. In some cases, they tell of aging parents still saying and doing cruel and destructive things to each other, with no end in sight. After a while, it becomes a way of life. The husband and wife would be lost without the ugly pain of their relationship. And these homes often give birth to those of the next generation which is also unable to function with any notion of what constitutes a healthy marriage. Their generation never saw one.

Hank and Alice are an example of the doormat marriage in which male dominance and female submissiveness cooperate toward the mutual destruction of both. There are infinite variations on this theme in which people manage to control, bully, or tyrannize the spouse to the satisfaction of the negative needs and impulses in each of them.

However, it should be remembered that this matrimonial hegemony is not exclusive to the male. The reign of the wife as tyrant or boss in the marriage is a familiar sight to counselors. The woman who "wears the pants" usually presides over her matriarchy and remains enthroned because her effete husband refuses to be his own man, insist on his rights, make message-clear decisions, and acting with strength and conviction.

A great explosion of laughter erupted from a large singles audience of both men and women once when I said that many men who are strong and autonomous at work arrive home at night with behavior that sounds like a little boy crying, "Mom-mie!" His questions to his wife cover the whole spectrum of his personal, as opposed to his vocational life: "Do you know where . . . why . . . what . . . when . . . who . . . ?" Every cry for help, even when camouflaged as information, can be felt by the partner as more dependency. The wife who has the answer has that much power. The first law of cybernetics, the study of systems, says that the entity within the system with the most options has the most power. If she is then given the power of decision and action in those areas, she ascends. If she is given command of most of the major areas of her husband's life, she is boss.

These questions are often subtly asked. They may be only implied by the flaccid personality of the male: (Do you know) *Where* my children are? *Why* my dog ignores me? *What* my values, needs, dreams are? *When* I may ever do anything? *Who* my friends are? The woman in charge has a "yes" for all of these and then proceeds to inform and propagandize the man. If he accepts her expertise in these matters, he is to that degree in her hands. We are not talking about mutual support and feedback, but rather the woman's systematic control of information and participation in the marriage in an effort to dominate the relationship. These women usually are demanding, loud, strong, tough, and generally officious.

More often, the ruling female is subtle and indirect, manipulating rather than plundering the man's decision and action systems. Again, we are not thinking here of the survival techniques to which women have traditionally been reduced due to the arrogance of men. I am speaking of the woman who *needs* to rule the man, either out of a neurotic fear or an enormous hostility, perhaps masked by the rules of female seductress or mother, either of which creates the "let me take care of you" atmosphere. She may come through as passive-aggressive; that is, she will not openly confront the man with an honest presentation of her feelings and ideas, but will use pouting, body complaints, denial of sex, and so forth, to get her way. Some people are even able to generate illness in order to influence their partners. This can be true of both men and women.

Emotional and physical abuse are not limited to either one sex or the other, even though, tragically, I have most often seen it in men, who abuse women rather than getting help for their own crippled egos. As we study families of origin, the roots of abuse usually become clear. Whether we speak of male or female abusers, it would seem that the original sin of our species is the abuse of children, from which comes a flood of evil and destruction in our lives, generation after generation. Only a great new preparation of parents for nurturing children can save us from our assault upon one another in the family.

Piggyback

One step away from the *doormat* marriage is the *piggyback* one. The motto here is "Carry me." One partner is in a dependent relationship to the other. One makes the decisions because the other is afraid, not of the partner, but of life. The "carrier" does most of the thinking and acting in the marriage; one partner feeds off the other. In a *piggyback* marriage, a psychologically crippled person is getting a very expensive ride. And, of course, this is the way the taxi partners want it; otherwise, they would change the situation. It may be the only way such persons can marry. One needs to be carried, and the other to carry. They may, however, profit from counseling.

Sally was a fifty-three-year-old nurse who came to me complaining about her husband who had become depressed after his father's death. "He sits around and does nothing. He is a good carpenter, but he's laying off work. When my daughter and her little girl come over, he goes into the bedroom and grumps. Our sex life has dropped off. He is picky and fussy about his food, and last Sunday evening he started to cry over some dumb show on TV. I've tried everything. He won't talk, play, go anywhere, or begin to think about Christmas with me. I'm scared."

She and Ed had two children, a son and a daughter, twenty-nine and twenty-seven, both divorced, and each with one child. The son was back at home, in his old room, complaining about everything, hating his job as an auto salesman when car sales had reached a new low, not dating much but out with the guys a lot. Their daughter had her own apartment, but Sally ran errands for her and often babysat on weekends even after a long week of nursing. The exploitative requests which the children made had no end, as Sally related incident after incident of "my children needing me."

As we talked, it became more and more clear that the entire

family had been "piggybacking" on Sally for years. She had always made herself totally accessible. She even tried to antici-
pate their needs, writing notes or reminders, making calls,
laying out clothes, leaving food prepared or cooking. She was in-
dispensable, the natural nurse, the supermom, feeding and
comforting those in her world.

Ed's new and deeper dependency was about to mobilize her
anger. She was beginning to resent and resist. She snapped and
crackled around the house, so that the two men were asking
each other in her presence, "What's with her?"

Toward the end of our first session as she paused to get her
breath after a long recitation of complaints and frustrations, I
asked, "And who takes care of you?" Her face went very dark
and her eyes filled as she said in a softer, higher, almost childlike
voice, "Nobody. Nobody ever did. Not even when I was a little
girl. Do you know that I practically raised my two little brothers? Dad died when I was eight and my mother went to work,
and I really became the mother to those kids. I fed and bathed
them. I took them to Sunday school while Mother stayed home
and slept in my clean house. I even rescued them from a small
fire we had once. (*Pause*) And you think I got any thanks? Oh, I
get cards at Christmas, but that's it. (*Pause*) You ask who takes
care of me? I do. Sometimes. I guess." She had been openly crying throughout all of this. Now she was sobbing, bent over,
daubing at her eyes with tissue, hurt and lonely.

As a child, Sally had learned "how to take care of," and she
got most of her strokes that way. It was almost as though she
was obsessively focused, both professionally and domestically,
on "looking after and nursing" her world. Since she was so capa-
ble and willing, people let her. Her profession was exciting and
rewarding for her, but she felt guilty about being away from the
family so much. So she doubled her efforts at home, making her
family even more dependent, robbing the others of their own autonomy, and leaving herself out.

There are two other important problems with this sort of relating. A person such as Sally gets most of her satisfaction indi-
rectly rather than directly. That is, she feels good only if
someone else feels good and not because something really nice
happens to her. It is hard to relate to this sort of person unless
you come for something, come with an empty cup so to speak,

and let them fill it for you. They spurn your approaching them to give or minister. *They* do the giving. Yet deep inside they are hungry and lonely.

After counseling, Sally did not break out in a dramatic confrontation with her family. She simply was less available to run errands, more direct about not having time or energy to take care of the comforts of her husband and son when they were clearly using her and not making an effort for themselves.

She used a creative innocence when they complained: "Oh, gee, I'm sorry I forgot to take care of that for you. Isn't it great that you were able to do it yourself?" More tartly when they angrily complained, she smiled, puckered her lips, and said, "Poor babee." They began to understand. Soon she was telling them that she had plans for the evening and would not be able to get the laundry done, so perhaps she should show them how to run the machines. On one of those evenings she simply went to her bedroom and curled up with a good novel.

She loved it. She felt she was playing a game, but it seemed to her a lot more healthy. Her friends and family were getting a strong, new message from Sally. Occasionally she delayed returning routine phone calls, declined church jobs, was not always available to substitute at the hospital or babysit for her daughter, and turned down invitations when she felt a need to be alone. She lost weight, began going regularly to a hairdresser, and bought some new clothes.

When she told Ed that she was in therapy, he was startled. She reported it to be a "good kick in the pants" for Ed. He quit pouting and withdrawing. His depression was lifting. He began taking her out to dinner and asked her to spend the weekend with him at a new hotel near the airport.

Ed even said he would be willing to see me if she wanted him to. She told him that it was up to him to decide. A couple of days later he called in to make his own appointment. At our first session Ed decided he had some things of his own to work on.

Piggyback is a marriage game that robs both partners of genuine autonomy and sets up powerful dependencies. It can create the "piggy" feelings of loneliness, resentment, and of being used. While the "rider" is pampered and indulged, he or she loses power, and may even despise the babying, not knowing how to protest without hurting the partner's feelings. A few searching questions for couples are these:

- If we are playing piggyback, which of us is which?
- When do I feel like "piggy" or "rider"? Do I like the feeling? What can I do about it?
- How exactly do you need me? And I you?
- How well could I survive without you? And you me?
- Do we rush to serve, protect, warn, or prepare each other?

Clutch

The *clutch* marriage is about two steps away from the *doormat* marriage. The motto here is, "Without you I would die." This couple is precariously balanced on the edge of things, holding on for dear life. It is similar to *piggyback* except there is no clearly strong individual. Both are passive, dependent, clinging persons who tiptoe through life, keep mostly to themselves, and are often pitifully alone even in marriage. Someone has described such a relationship this way: the rocks in his head fit the holes in hers.

Jean and Harvey were referred to me by their pastor. In response to my inquiry as to why they had come, Jean, a thin woman, poorly groomed, said, "First, we want you to know that we are decent people. What happened had nothing to do with the kind of people we are. We love each other, and we are going to be all right. We talked with our pastor, and he thought we ought to see you at least once. So we are here."

She continued telling me that she never wanted to be anything but a good wife and mother. She played the piano at the Sunday school and liked to read "inspirational writers." She finished her introduction by turning to Harvey and saying, "Why don't you tell the doctor a little about you now, so he will know what kind of folks we are."

Harvey taught history at a community college, but he admitted that he did not like his students, "who won't read, can't write, and talk too much." Out of class he mostly read, listened to the classical music radio station, played chess with Jean, and wrote scholarly articles about local history that were seldom published. Harvey was considerably overweight. He ushered in a neighborhood church. He said that he and Jean did not drink or smoke and seldom went to the movies because most of them were "not fit for human consumption." Public television was okay.

There was a pause and I suggested once more that they tell me why their pastor had referred them. Jean began again by describing for me their four-year-old daughter, Rebecca, "who pretty much runs things at our house." She related an embarrassing story about the child's public tantrums.

"Well, last Sunday evening I caught Harvey playing with Rebecca in the tub." She described what she had seen. She had not interrupted the sexual play, but later confronted Harvey with what she had seen. Harvey denied it. She asked him to go with her to talk with their pastor. He consented, but again denied Jean's accusation. At that point in her story I glanced at Harvey just as he broke into tears and flung himself into Jean's lap. He sobbed that he was a terrible father, who did not deserve her or Rebecca.

With this, Jean began to stroke his hair and comfort him. She then pulled him up to her and rocked him like a baby. He soon sat up, told her what a wonderful wife she was, and that she should not worry, that he would never disappoint her again. They smiled longingly at each other, and Harvey turned to me to announce that they very much appreciated my help, and now would not need to return.

I tried to ask questions about what was happening. "Are you saying you do not feel a need to pursue this further?"

"I don't see why," he said, wiping his eyes. "What do you think, honey?"

"I agree," Jean answered, nodding her head.

I pushed a bit. "Wouldn't you like to explore what was going on in this incident?"

"Oh, I think I understand it," said Harvey. "I just lost control for a moment. And as I just promised Jean (he smiled at her), that will never happen again." He paused briefly. "You believe me, don't you, honey?"

"Certainly, I do," she said.

Again I asked, "Do you feel that what happened could in any way reflect what is going on in your marriage?"

This time Jean answered, "Why, what do you mean? We have

one of the best marriages I know of. I hope you don't think we don't have good sex relations because of what happened. No, Doctor, you are wrong there."

Harvey followed quickly, "We get along fine in bed. Neither of us ever had an affair, and we have a happy home."

"What about your little girl?"

He continued, "She'll be fine. We love her an awful lot and she knows it. Love and limits. That's what children need. She has the love. We just have to work on the limits a bit."

This was a marriage of quiet desperation. The incident with the child was another symptom of the immaturity and boredom evidenced throughout the family. They were not only poorly involved in life but also were tragically caught in the emotional webs of the marriage, as demonstrated by Jean's rushing quickly to the defense of their sex life, even when it was not directly under attack. There was finally an emotional confession, easy forgiveness, and a promise with automatic acceptance. It was as though "Mommie" had caught her little boy misbehaving; yet he was quickly reinstated into her good graces because both saw the event as a moral issue rather than an emotional conflict, and moral issues were answered with judgment, confession, and forgiveness. Emotional issues require self-searching, a look at the context in which the problem rests, causes, reasons, options, and understanding, so that behavior becomes a reasoned and rewarding thing, rather than merely controlled.

Harvey was disenchanted with his vocation. Jean appeared satisfied with her life as wife and mother; yet both husband and daughter (with her tantrums) were acting out. For this marriage and family to heal would require considerable work; yet there were indications that, with courage, Harvey and Jean could grow. The marriage seemed tight, fixed, simplistic, and uninspired, caught in routine, and doomed to more incestuous incidents in quest of any kind of "turn-on." While not a picture of hope, such a marriage is not necessarily terminally ill if the couple can heed the symptoms and get to work on them.

When I told Jean and Harvey that by law the incident would have to be reported to the authorities, they were devastated. Only then did they exhibit any real sense of the gravity of the event and of the general health of their marriage and family. Then we were able to get down to a serious discussion of the work that lay ahead for them. A sense of relief and a flicker of hope were more and more apparent as we moved toward the end of their first of many sessions in their long journey into health.

Idol

The motto of the *idol* marriage is "Worship me." One partner considers himself or herself to be worthy of very special attention. The superperson wants lots of praise for beauty, talent, brains, money, or whatever. The other can only stand in awe, shrink in public, and lead the ovation with friends. It is a tiresome marriage. Most often it is the wife who worships. She begins every social event with a "Guess what my marvelous husband has done now?" sort of invitation. You're a good friend according to how extravagantly you guess: "A $10,000 bonus?" "Promoted to president?" "He's jogging!"

An *idol* marriage is another form of slavery. The spouse who insists on being idolized is probably suffering from narcissism. Narcissus, in Greek mythology, was a handsome young man who fell in love with his own reflection in a pool and pined away until he fell in and drowned. In a marriage in which there is the worshiped and the worshiper, the first insists on special privilege, deference, and inordinate expressions of gratitude and adoration. The other feels fortunate to be able to participate in such a marriage. For the worshiping partner, it is a great honor to serve and share the limelight with this marvelous mate.

Lloyd and Jackie were in their early thirties and had been married five years. They made a handsome couple. He was an airline executive, and she had been a hostess when Lloyd met and married her. He insisted that she quit work and keep their townhouse, stay in shape with a spa membership, and generally run errands for him and his horses. Most of his free time was spent caring for, training, and showing horses. Jackie was allowed to do very little directly for the horses, nor could she ride them. She was forbidden to buy her own horse. Lloyd did not want any but purebreds, and they were too expensive for Jackie to use simply for pleasure. She continued to assist him and sacrificed her own desire for a horse. She suggested finally that she be allowed to get a riding horse and keep it at another stable. Lloyd was annoyed. It was his hobby, his very serious hobby.

He did not want to be distracted from purebred horses, and he did not want her energy going elsewhere. But he did not suggest any solution except to say, "Why can't you just enjoy what I am doing with horses?" Most of their money went into his hobby.

When Jackie came for her first appointment, she complained of migraine headaches, feeling jittery, not being able to sleep, and worrying her mother with all the Valium she was taking. "I never feel like eating," she said, "although I do find myself into cookies or chips sometimes before I even realize what I'm doing. But with Lloyd the way he is, I could never allow myself to gain weight." She laughed. "I think he'd divorce me over five pounds in the wrong places."

"What do you do when you can't sleep?" I asked.

"Well, let's see. Last night I got up and sewed. I'm making Lloyd's shirt for the show. He looks so great up there on that big horse. You can almost hear the women 'ooh' and 'aah' when he rides out." She laughed nervously. "I really expect them to swoon. He said one did last time, but I didn't see it. I dunno. Maybe. He's beautiful."

"What about you, Jackie? Where do you see things going for you?" I queried.

"Me? Wherever Lloyd goes, I guess. Doing things for him. He calls me his maidservant. 'Hey, maidservant,' he'll say, 'get me my whatchama-call-it." And I go flying. It's really a sort of honor for me to be on his team. Then it's show time, and he's out there riding, looking like a god, and I say under my breath, 'He's mine, all mine, girls. So hands off.' " She was visibly excited.

"What's he like otherwise?" I inquired. "You know, away from the horses, just around the house?"

"Oh, there. Well, he's rather a loner. Of course, he's at the stables a lot – or on the phone, or going to see someone about horses. He exercises, swims, keeps himself in perfect condition. No hobbies but horses. He reads books and magazines about horses, mostly just before bed. He even reads fiction about horses."

"Okay. But what about you? What are you doing all this time?"

"Oh, things. Cleaning house, laundry, food. Lloyd likes good food, special dishes. I sew. I've learned to make all his show outfits. And they are gorgeous. Lloyd says it's the best thing I do. It would cost a fortune to buy what I can make. That's how it started. My mother sews, and I never sewed a thing until once she suggested I do it when I told her how much Lloyd wanted a certain jacket that was really expensive. A hand-stitched thing, embroidery, the works. My mother and I made it. Well, I helped her. But now I do it all. Anyway, I gave it to him for his birthday that year, and did he ever love it!"

I leaned forward. "Okay, now *you*. Tell me about *you*. Are you only Lloyd's maidservant?"

She laughed. "Oh, goodness, no. I read nights mostly. Watch a little TV when Lloyd is busy. Visit my mom. Recently I've gotten into plants some, too."

"Do you have your own friends?"

"Oh, yeah, sure. There are a couple of other girls whose husbands are also into horses. I see them sometimes – lunch, a movie. I went to an art exhibition with Vi. Mostly I see the girls when we go out of town to do a show. We all go together, three couples. We get a bunch of rooms at a motel. We have fun drinking and dancing after the show, unless Lloyd wants to get to bed so we can hit the road early for home."

Her whole life was Lloyd and the horses. I could not find her outside her servitude. "What did you want to do before you met Lloyd?" I asked.

"Fly. I always wanted to fly – since I was little. I mean really little, like four of five."

"And how long were you a hostess?"

"Four years."

"Will you ever go back to that?"

"I doubt it. Why should I?"

"But you wanted that for so long!"

"Oh, yes. But that was 'BL,' before Lloyd." She smiled. There was a pause.

"Will you have a family? Do you want children?"

"I do. Lloyd doesn't. At least I thought I did. The more I see and hear about kids, the more I think I'm glad my man doesn't want any. Lloyd said just the other day that a poll showed that couples without kids were happier than those with them."

The session closed with my asking if she thought Lloyd would come in to see me. She said she thought he might. Her mother had advised her to see me when she told her about her body complaints. She would ask Lloyd that night and let me know. She said she felt better and wanted to make another appointment for herself for later that same week.

The next morning my secretary said that her husband had called in and canceled Jackie's appointment. When my secretary asked if she might give me the reason for the cancellation, he said he thought his chiropractor could handle the situation.

Two months later Jackie was back in my office on her mother's arm. Lloyd was furious and had ordered her to file for divorce if she returned to see me. After months of hard work and the divorce, Jackie was a different person and considering nursing school. She still wanted to serve, but she had a deeper understanding of her own emotional needs, greater self-esteem and autonomy, and clearer personal goals that were hers for *her* life.

Over the years of my practice there have been many similar marital arrangements. Briefly, here are two others.

There was the man whose mother was killed in an auto accident when he was six. His father remarried, and his second mother died of cancer when he was fifteen. He was married when he was twenty-seven to a woman eight years his senior, with two small children. He became her "third child" and he shamelessly worshiped her. The problem was that she came to resent his "weakness and baby talk" and the fact that she was responsible for the business and recreation of the entire family. By the time they came to me, she was involved in an affair, which he knew about. He told her that he was able to handle it if she needed that. Privately to me he said, "I can't let a little thing like an affair spoil our marriage. She'll be back. She did the last time. This is one fantastic woman. I guess she could do about anything she wants, and I don't think I would really object. She is wise and fair, and she would not be doing this if there were not some deep need." They were finally divorced, and he moved in with his father, where he has remained unmarried, and without therapy. It is very hard for a mate to feel like an adult spouse in a peer relationship when she feels like the only grown-up in the house.

An older couple came to see me after thirty-seven years of his worshiping her. They finally hit a snag when she wanted him to retire at sixty from work that he deeply enjoyed and move to California to be near their daughter. She said, "Why is it that you have to be so stubborn after all these years?" Privately he shared a letter with me that he had received from his daughter, who said she and her husband did not want her mother living nearby. The letter concluded with: "You, of all people, should know how mother is – always right, demanding attention. She thinks she's the Virgin Mary. Do whatever you have to, Daddy, but keep her there. If you don't, I swear that Phil and I will move to Australia." After a number of sessions, the worshiping husband turned agnostic. He and his daughter confronted his wife, who decided that being loved was better than being worshiped, and the couple remained where they were.

Hide-and-Seek

The motto of the *hide-and seek* marriage is, "Where are you?" In marriages like these, the spouse tries to keep the mate guessing. She or he is a mystery: busy, hidden, vague, and always somehow not quite satisfied with the spouse. The partner never knows where he or she stands, feels off-balance, with the other perhaps subtly threatening to "lower the boom" if the partner is not careful. And on top of it all, the seeking spouse is encouraged to "try to understand how I feel" and asked, "Why do you say that I avoid you?" This is followed by, "I don't know why you seem to find me difficult and strange. The folks at the office think I'm okay. *They* like me!"

Geri and Tom had been married almost sixteen years when Geri came to see me. She was a tall, slim woman and an attractive mother of two teenage girls. Her deferring nature was immediately apparent as we met: "I know you are a very busy man, and I am sorry to take your time. Besides, I doubt whether you or anyone can tell me what to do about my situation. Anyway, it's been going on for so long, I wonder if we could change it if we tried."

She paused for a quick, tight smile and a long sigh. "My mother says I am lucky to have him. Tom. That he is a better man than my father was. He's dead. And I should just look around at my neighbors. One is divorced, and another deserted. Even our minister is leaving his wife, I think. (*Pause*) It really is me, I guess. At least Mother and Tom and the girls seem to think so. They laugh at me. Tom says it's a wonder sometimes he comes home at all. (*Pause*) Sometimes I feel I am being ignored. I ask them to do something and it gets half-done. Come to think of it, everything in my life seems half done. We never did really finish off the basement. Kids played in it when they were little but we never use it now. And it's all that way. Half-done. I'm the only one that goes to church anymore. Tom never did except on special days, or when the girls were doing something they wanted him to attend. Half-done. That's really funny. Dishes, beds, washing, lessons. Even our sex life. I never thought of it before. Tom and I never enjoy it together. We aren't lovers. It's as though one night it's for him and another night it's for me, according to how we feel. Who's tired, or whatever."

She laughed. Amused and with the charm of a child who has made a discovery, she said, "Yep. I have a half-baked life all right." The laugh was now more cynical. "And guess who does the other half, the half they leave, the part they hate?" There was a long pause as she looked away, staring.

"Does Tom help?" I ventured.

"Tom? *Him*? Heaven's no! But then, why should he? He works hard and provides quite well for us." She looked back at me.

"You want to tell me about Tom?"

"I'll be glad to. He's forty-one, tall, dark, and handsome. Very athletic. Does not drink or smoke. Loves foreign cars. Plays a grand piano, and has been top banana in his agency for the past six years, and among the top in the whole nation. He's great. No doubt about it. He is courteous, thoughtful, and generous. A good scout. Last year for my birthday he sent me to Hawaii to see my brother." She paused again and her eyes filled. "It's just that he is gone all the time. He's in an auto club, a flying club, and of course there is all the stuff that goes on at his tennis club. He has breakfast meetings, plays handball at lunch, swims one night a week, and mixes in golf and tennis in good weather. Plus, of course, there are all the local teams and their games. Late nights he reads reports and things. And all this after many nights of two or three appointments. He can mix work and play better than any one I know."

"Would you say that even his play sounds like work?" I asked.

"Well, maybe," she answered. "But he seems to love it all. And the girls are just as bad. Kim is in everything at school. Every group she's in is always calling to find her. (*She laughed.*) And she's always somewhere else. Sue's the senior. Has her own car and is a nurse's aide after school. She wants to be a nurse. But I never see her either. She has this great dating life going and says she'll never marry. I don't know. They're all so busy. Is that good?" I raised my brow. She smiled sadly.

"What about you?" I asked.

"Me? Well, there's the trouble. I don't have the energy they do. I just can't keep up. I had rheumatic fever when I was eight and I've never been the same. Even when the girls were tiny, they exhausted me. Doctors say I am fine. No scars on the heart or anything. (*She laughed.*) But *I* say I have never been the same. (*Pause*) Tom agrees. He says I'm not as strong even as when we married. I was twenty then. Of course he was always doing things I couldn't. Swimming, biking, skating. We did dance a little, but I tired so quickly. But I do try. We are members of a dinner club, and we go there faithfully, every first Saturday night. I enjoy that if we leave early enough. It's hard to tear Tom away before midnight. I turn into a pumpkin at midnight."

"You mentioned the choir."

"Oh, yes. I do that, but I'm the quietest little soprano there. After a special choir program, like the Christmas cantata, I'm exhausted."

"What else do you and Tom do?"

"Not much actually. (*Pause*) We almost never have sex anymore. I guess that's what got me here today. He complains. I'm too skinny, too whiny, too slow. Too something. Or he's tired. That's a switch, isn't it? The guy tired. (*Pause*) But it used to be good. (*She smiled.*) Well . . . , pretty good. I was never a Mata Hari. I still like to lie close to him though. Sometimes he lets me scratch his back until he goes to sleep. Sometimes I just lie there and watch him sleep. Guess I'm just hungry for the sight of him." She laughed and her eyes filled.

"What does the laugh say?"

She was embarrassed. "Oh, I don't know. It sounded silly to say I was hungry for the sight of a man who was lying there asleep on his stomach with his face to the wall."

She had talked for some time, and I sensed it could go on forever with all of her complaints falling flat as she laughed at her needs and put herself down with quotes from Mother, Tom, and the girls. So I gave her a note pad and asked her to draw a picture of the way she felt about her life. After the usual jokes about not being an artist, she became quiet and closed her eyes to get the picture. In a few moments tears began again. She opened her eyes and, blotting them with a Kleenex, began to draw.

She explained her drawing. "That's me – up a tree. The bear is my fears. I'm scared. Tom and the girls are in the jet flying away and leaving me out on a limb over a cliff." She was very clear about her condition.

In subsequent sessions we spent time working on Geri's self-image. After a complete physical examination, she was told that she was in excellent health, except for her weight, which was too light, and could exercise as she chose. Soon she joined a therapy group and was supported in an expanding program of self-enhancing activities. She changed her hairstyle and grooming, began reading and watching programs on the public television station, and started a course in guitar. Since she did not work out of the home, she began attending a variety of programs in the city.

She confronted her family more. When things were half done, they were told to redo them. She asked Tom about having the basement completed so they could use it to entertain. He put her off. So she called three companies in town for estimates. Tom then took time to plan with her, ordered materials, and the two of them went to work on the basement. She began giving small dinner parties with two other couples, and Tom was there in his own inimitable style as host. She put together her own little crash "Eliza Doolittle program." There was no heavy, torturous therapy – just a decision to risk something. The depression lifted as she liked herself better.

By this time the family knew she was up to something. They believed she was just going to "another church meeting" when she came to the group. The family hardly missed her. But they knew she was different. She said she was praying harder. Actually she was doing that, too.

Then in the spring, Tom won a trip to Miami and he asked her to go along. This time she did. Before, she would have used the excuse that the girls needed her, and Tom would have agreed. They had a great time together. She reported to the group: "Good food. I gained three pounds. Good fun. And good sex." She was getting into Tom's world as much as possible, and he began to participate in hers. She then told Tom she wanted her own sports car. Tom was surprised, then angry, and finally amused. "Nothing fancy," she said, "just a small, yellow convertible." She got it, and Tom spent an entire weekend with her, giving her pointers, while she did the driving. "After my old klunker," she said, "this little beauty is enough to make a gal leave home."

Things were better than Geri could ever remember them. The girls still went their own way, but they helped more and took her more seriously. "Actually, I'm sort of glad they're growing away from us. I want to concentrate on Tom," she said. When she asserted herself, the girls just stared at her, shook their heads, and did as she asked. Geri was even able to remind her mother that she was not a child and Mother might very well learn to keep some of her opinions to herself. Mother did not telephone for two full days; then she called to say "You've changed, and I don't like it. Are you going to those women's lib meetings?"

The marriage really began to move, however, when Geri announced to Tom that she was enrolled in a flying course and expected to be able to "have the family plane for heavy dates." She had thought to surprise him one day at the airport by offering to pilot the plane on one of their trips but decided that was "too cutesy."

Soon afterwards Geri left the group. She was becoming a beautiful, strong, autonomous woman, who was living out her life with a lot of satisfaction. Also, she and Tom were friends, talking and sharing. Their partnership was one of equals, with a contract that Geri would not take a job. She said, with a slight, becoming arrogance, "I'm too busy."

She had accepted volunteer jobs at her church and a gallery. She and Tom were lovers. Their sex life was much improved. She was teasing Tom about getting a vasectomy.

It sounds like a fairy tale, too good to be true. Actually, it was even better than this account can suggest. Once Geri decided that *she* was her problem and began to take herself seriously in

every way, she was able to reconstruct her marriage. Confront-
ing Tom would have been calamitous. She had been dull and
complaining. She had been afraid. She had *needed* them. They
did not need her as she was prepared to be needed, but they
used her because the role of "Mommie" was all she had to offer.
In fact, she was a drag. Her own growth was personal and permanent. She was marvelous to watch. Everyone felt the impact
of the shy, tired female becoming a head-up, happy woman. I
never met Tom. She wanted it that way.

Seesaw

The *seesaw* marriage is a face-to-face relationship, observed
and observing. There is closeness with distance; the gap can be
closed for deeper intimacy. I can recall standing up with my
partner on a seesaw, holding hands across the fulcrum, and with
a little knee action having a few moments of fun until we fell.
The seesaw model suggests an interesting aspect of a dialogical
relationship. It is an interdependent model. Each needs the
other in order to seesaw. Yet, one has the good feeling of carrying his or her own weight – lifting, the waiting, rising, and falling in an undulating rhythm, responsive and responsible. If one
slides up toward the center, it is even possible to "coast" for a
while, feet up, eyes closed, while the watchful partner provides
the energy and monitors the rhythm, "taking care of" the other.
Every analogy finally breaks down. So does the seesaw. Yet it
comes closer than most to suggesting many of the mutual and
reciprocal elements of a healthy marriage. We shall attempt in
the following chapters to set forth what appear to be the necessary elements of the seesaw model of marriage between autonomous adults.

Before you proceed, it may be helpful to create your own
model. Perhaps it is at first only a simple cartoon like Geri's as a
way of getting at what it feels like to be in your marriage. Often
it is useful to model in order to uncover buried feelings and attitudes. Once a group of couples used boxes of Tinkertoys to build
models of their marriages. Some worked together, others apart.
Some argued and struggled over favorite pieces. One man took
over and built while his wife passively watched. Another pouted
and withdrew when his wife accused him of being "too slow and

unimaginative." The process was illuminating. The feelings flowed. All agreed that the exercise was in some poignant ways reflective of things that went on in their marriage. Take a few minutes to get a mental picture of how you feel about your marriage. Now draw a picture of it. If you can, share it with your mate. Invite him or her to draw a picture also and discuss the picture. How do they make you feel about life together?

As we move from thinking about autonomy to a consideration of intimacy in the chapters on friends, partners, and lovers, perhaps one more abstract picture we would draw of our marriage is this:

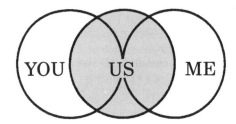

The plane of the seesaw goes through these circles. As the seesaw goes up and down, each carries and is carried. This represents not the dependency of childhood, nor the independence of adolescence, but the *interdependence* of adulthood. We need one another; but more, we *want* to do life together. As the seesaw moves up and down, as we carry each other's burdens, at the mid-point each time we are on the same plane together, we are peers looking into each other's eyes as absolute equals.

As autonomous adults we must be about realizing our own destiny evolving out of our own inner dialogue. I need time with myself to discover and enable the person I want to become. We must encourage each other in these talks.

As intimate adults we must be about getting each other loved, so that we truly feel loved by our mate. This means that there must be time, place and energy for the outer dialogue of the marriage so that our relationship is also realized.

A marriage requires a delicate balance among these three arenas: you, me and us. No one of them can be larger than the other for long or the relationship suffers. The *us* often takes over as when the family becomes more important than the couple's relationship. This is indeed typical in our society. The family looks great. The marriage looks good, but the personal, intimate relationship between the couple is terrible. They have forgotten why they got married in the first place. Unless they heal their relationship the marriage and family will die. If the relationship does not come first, there may be no family. In fact, divorces most often come because the couple dies as a couple and thus the family is destroyed. As couples we must constantly renew our commitment.

Keep the seesaw in mind as you talk together. It suggests equality, commitment, support, cooperation and the delicate balance between *autonomy* and *intimacy*, the two poles of any covenant relationship. I must love me. You must love you. And we must truly love one another. Then we are connected and integrated as the circles suggest.

If you drew these circles now the way you feel you are connected, how would they look? Floating in space? Piled on top of each other? What is your balance of autonomy and intimacy?

Chapter 3

THE FRIENDSHIP OF MARRIAGE

Friendship is the foundation of adult marriage. When two people find each other in this world of so many chance meetings, when they risk disclosing themselves, come to care deeply about one another in all the when, where, how, and why of life, and make a living thing of closeness, we have an impressive event. If they go deeper to confront one another with their closeness, believing in the survival of their love though it be driven to the wall, we have a miracle. But when that man and woman create a friendship together and add, "I want to spend my life with you," we have something more impressive than any miracle. We have the first phase of perhaps the greatest drama of the human saga, in which most of all what it means to be man and woman is searched and tested, tried and celebrated, in anguish and joy. If this sounds utopian, visionary, and like nothing you ever see, it is still worth watching for and working for in our lonely time.

The Need to Know and Be Known

Definitions of the healthy personality often include lists and descriptions of what may be called basic human needs. One need badly overlooked is *the need to be known* as an essential characteristic of the mature adult. We see that need expressed everywhere. It is the first ingredient of friendship – the beginning of any significant relationship.

A friend visits a social group or a church, is ignored, and complains, "No one even knew I was there." She was not acknowledged as being present, the first step in knowing.

A teenager erupts at a negligent parent, "I'm your daughter, but you don't know me at all. You don't know anything about me. You barely know my name."

Creation begins in the Bible with naming: heaven, earth, waters, darkness, light, evening and morning, and the first day. All are given names: Adam, Eve, animals, birds, and plants. Infants learn to name: Dada, Mama. Naming is the first act of language, and perhaps the deepest sense of knowing. Little children make the connection. The five-year-old daughter of our friends joyfully declared to her parents after her baptism: "Now God knows my name." The ritual represented a special moment of recognition.

The Hebrew language uses the same word for knowing with the mind and the sexual experiencing of another person in intercourse. *To know* suggests a profound awareness of another with a depth and intimacy that is extraordinary.

A couple said to me, "We lived on that street for almost two years, and never really got to know anybody there. Oh, we spoke when we went out to get the paper, and once when everybody came out to watch firemen get a cat out of the tree. But getting to know people takes effort."

A man once told me, "I want to smoke the biggest cigar and drive the biggest car this side of the Anacostia River. I want people to know who I am."

Eric Berne, creator of the term "transactional analysis," has written a book entitled *What Do You Say After You Say Hello?* "Hello" is the first step in the hazardous and miraculous movement toward intimacy, toward being deeply known by another. A friendship begins with a need to be known. Perhaps this even somehow precedes the need to be loved; certainly chronologically and in fact it must. But in some ways the need to be known by another may be the primary psychological and social need. Indeed, it also appears at the heart of every great religion: the need to be truly known by God and still loved in spite of ourselves. The concept of *imago dei*, suggests that we are created in the image of God and are therefore recognized, known as God's creation and hence of supreme value. It is the foundation of our democracy. Our "inalienable rights" are endowed by our creator who knows us as his own. We are all kin to one another in that great knowing.

We do not have to argue for the primacy of the need to be known over the need to be loved. We are reminded that it is not possible to be loved until we are known. Becoming known is simply a necessary step toward becoming loved. Be that as it may, even when we are loved, and when we do not expect the whole sequence of known-to-loved to develop in a new relationship, we still enjoy being known. We like to be introduced and have someone say with obvious delight, "Oh, I know who you are."

Many of the emotional conflicts that we find in people have to do with the fear of being known. If you know me, you can control me. If you know me, you may find that I am bad or stupid or empty – whatever my fear is. If you know me, you will know my weakness, and you will hurt me. If I let you know me, then I feel obligated to get to know you, and I am committed to a relationship which frightens me.

Some years ago, J. William Pfeiffer and John E. Jones gave us the "Joharie" window in their book *A Handbook of Structured Experiences for Human Relations Training*. It looks like this:

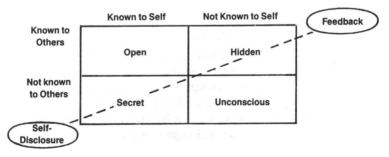

In quadrant one we have the *open* area of the person, those things clearly available, known to self and to others, and as obvious as size, color of hair, and color of eyes – that which is apparent.

In quadrant two is the *hidden* aspect, self, which is called the "bad breath" area. Robert Burns spoke of this area when he suggested what a gift it would be if we could see ourselves as others see us.

In quadrant three are the *secrets*, that which we cover and protect: bits of history, our fears and failures, dreams and loves, things we are shy about revealing or are ashamed of, or even things that give us a secret delight.

In quadrant four are all the elements of the *unconscious*, buried by time or will, locked out of awareness. It is this part of the self that Freud and others have uncovered with hypnosis, free association, dreams, fantasies, jokes, and slips of the tongue. It is a fascinating underworld of all sorts of materials. Freud thought the unconscious contained mostly the ugly and unhappy personal experiences that the conscious mind declined to hold and thus buried. Carl Jung said that there are also some good things there, symbols of the entire human experience.

The unconscious is both a private and a human-family collection of historical fragments, symbols (fire, rainbow), myths (generation, salvation stories), archetypes (Mother, Father, Hero), intuitions, fantasies, energies, and dreams forgotten. It is like a computer, seemingly able to summon almost any combination of words, sounds, feelings, actions, and visions that the mind can contain and flash them across the screen of the mind with terror or delight, in dream or fantasy, to inform or obscure reality. It was Elias Howe's dream of a knight snatching a lady's scarf and threading it through the eye in the point of his lance that gave him the idea of the sewing machine needle, which pushes rather than pulls the thread through the cloth. Many believe that it is in the unconscious that the ultimate direction of one's life is being determined day by day – below the level of consciousness where a profound and subtle mixing and sorting of one's total experience is constantly occurring, winsomely or tyrannically, to lead us down the paths of our destiny.

The process of *becoming known* by another is dialogical. It occurs in the interpersonal exchange of impressions, ideas, feelings, and values as people get acquainted. In the second quadrant of the window, it may be seen by another that my jacket is torn or that I ignored a red traffic light, neither of which I realized until someone who cared was willing to tell me. In the third quadrant I became known as I disclosed that German chocolate is my favorite cake; that it annoyed me to have my wife tell me I missed the traffic signal; and that I prefer playing to watching baseball. In the fourth quadrant I am revealed in the telling of a dream or fantasy, in a slip of the tongue, or in a painting of mine that a friend interprets.

We become known in all four quadrants. *Dialogue* is the process of self-disclosure and feedback suggested by the broken diagonal line connecting *self-disclosure* and *feedback* in the diagram. It is in this process that a relationship grows in what Martin Buber calls the in-betweenness of the I-Thou experience. The ability to self-disclose and handle feedback freely and appropriately with another, so that an in-betweenness (an us-ness) emerges in which understanding, respect, and love can flourish, is an essential mark of emotional health and maturity.

In fact, it is the quality of the dialogue that is the hallmark of any great intimacy between friends, partners, and lovers, or parents and children, or creature and creator. At the heart of intimacy is an ongoing dialogue of disclosure, sharing who we are. A woman once said to her husband in my office, "I'm stopping sex with you as of right now." As her startled husband tried to recover she continued, "because after fourteen years of marriage I just realized that I don't know you anymore. I don't know what you are thinking, feeling, or doing most of the time. I don't really know what you care about." Then she paused and concluded without a smile, "And I don't go to bed with strangers."

It is in dialogue that communication occurs. To communicate is to talk and touch. We may also whistle, wink, frown, draw pictures, or rely on ESP. Even body language is itself a language, and hence a kind of talk. In transactional analysis we speak of giving someone positive or negative strokes, so that even touching is talking and vice versa. It may be that the most reassuring touch of all is a warm hug, and the deepest word to be communicated is *closeness*, which describes a quality of love most of us seek.

If we have a reciprocal need to be known and this gives pleasure, we will take special care that our need and pleasure are satisfied by creating a mutual closeness. However, if our need and pleasure transcend all other needs, we may sacrifice our integrity in order to get closeness. It is then that trust is jeopardized. If both parties withhold truth for the sake of closeness, the relationship will last only as long as neither party has a greater need for truth than for closeness.

Perhaps it goes without saying that once we decide to disclose ourselves, the next hardest part of the dialogue is to receive the feedback without being defensive. To truly listen, receive, and learn from your mate's feedback is an enormous challenge. But we must keep in mind that real communication demands it. A defensive mate discourages honesty and prevents growth.

The Need to Trust and Be Trusted

In a healthy friendship there is a need to trust and to be trusted. Erik Erikson in his book *Childhood and Society*, says that trust or distrust is the first thing the infant learns in the initial eighteen months of life. Trust is life's foundation stone. All else proceeds from the quality of our trusting. Our earliest experiences condition our ability to trust and thus profoundly influence our relationships. In the disclose/feedback movement toward closeness, a need to trust is paramount. We must be certain that the message between us is authentic and understood. As the dialogue expands from the first *hello*, trust begins to form from words, body expressions, and the reasonableness of our story. We tell ourselves with a cluster of signals, trusting the receiver to be open and fair, not expecting double proof: that is, not only to prove my credibility, but also to disprove the other's prejudice or hang-up about *all* men, *all* women, *all* psychologists, and so forth. It is the double-proof syndrome that often sabotages relationships at the outset. For trust to develop, we must be able to check it out (by raising questions in order to verify our assumptions or feelings) as well as to give feedback.

Jim and Sue are concluding dinner together a week after they met.

Jim: "You know, I think it takes a lot of courage to be able to come right out and tell me that you are seeing a psychologist."

Sue: "Really?" (*Here we go again. He thinks I'm nuts.*)

Jim: "Yeah. I don't think most people would. I wouldn't. At least not on the first date."

Sue: "Why not? There's nothing to be ashamed of." (*On which date would he like to be told? Number two, number nineteen?*)

Jim: "Oh, I didn't mean to imply that there is. I guess I just feel it takes guts to admit to it on the first date. It's not like I'm a total stranger, but you hardly know me, and . . . "

Sue: "Look! Cut it, will you? I *know* how you feel. You've certainly made that clear. I'm sorry I even brought the subject up. You obviously feel that anyone who goes to a shrink is crazy. For your information, I started therapy to find out why I get involved with weak, dependent men who drink too much. And after seeing you inhale those two martinis before dinner, it looks as though my choice has not improved."

The first hazard is building trust in the double-proof washout. Here Sue not only requires that Jim sound believable, but he must also carefully avoid the innuendo and allusion that fits her own stereotype. Had she not been so defensive, she might have checked out why he felt she had courage, rather than assuming that he was implying that therapy is such an awful thing that its disclosure should be saved till later in the relationship.

It might have gone this way with a little more care on Sue's part.

Jim: "You know, I think it takes a lot of guts for you to be able to just come right out and tell me that you are seeing a shrink."

Sue: "Really? Why do you say that?"

Jim: "Oh, I don't know. I just don't think most people would. I wouldn't. At least not on the first date."

Sue (smiling): "Well, on which date would you prefer I tell you?"

Jim (laughing): "Oh, I didn't mean it that way. I just think it's

really neat that you are so open. I don't let people in like
that. I wish I could. They say I am hard to get to know.
You think that's true?"

Sue: "Well, I don't know. From what you just said I think you
are doing very well letting me know how you see yourself.
You seem to feel you are stand-offish, and it seems that
some people have confirmed that. You're letting me in."

Jim: "Thanks. That's really nice. You know, it really is easy to
talk with you. Gee, I don't know, maybe I could have told
you on the first date that I was seeing a shrink."

Both were laughing.

The first dialogue was actually reported to me by the woman
who told Jim off and later regretted her response. She herself
role-played the second dialogue in my office. Afterwards she
said, "I was more eager to prove him a bastard than to understand him, and I turned out to be a bitch instead."

She asked Jim to share a coffee break with her and checked
out her role-play by asking with a smile, "What were you *really*
trying to say to me the other night before I jumped on you?"
His response was remarkably what she had put together in her
fantasy. She came back pleased that she, at least, had been able
to fantasize the healthier dialogue.

Trust is built like a stone foundation for a house. The base is
dug in and the stones are fitted stone upon stone, great ones
and small ones, each in what seems to be its own, special place,
so that little mortar is necessary in order for the foundation to
stand. There is self-disclosure and feedback, no double-proof-
ing. Check it out and make the circle: another stone in place.
Slowly but surely more and more is trusted to the other. We become trusted and trusting. The stones are carefully put in place,
each one bringing another stone of trust and another, until the
foundation is secure.

One of our family's most special experiences was the time we
built a stone retaining wall across the front of the sloping yard
of our very first family home in Storrs, Connecticut. Discussing
what size and shape was needed, finding just the right stone,
helping each other to put it in place, and admiring our work together was a wonderful dialogue. It was not without dispute,
but was a good exercise in building trust.

The Need to Accept and Be Accepted

In a letter to Carl Jung on December 6, 1906, Frankl said that the basis of his new "talking cure" – psychoanalysis – was love. Carl Rogers speaks of a counselor having *unconditional positive regard* for his client if there is to be rapport between them. To be accepted is to be seen as a person of worth, to be treated as one who does not have to prove that she or he is of value. A husband once said to his wife, "I will love you when you lose weight." She replied, "When you love me, I will lose weight." Neither felt accepted simply for who he or she was. Each felt unacceptable to the other. He was really saying, "If you loved me, you would lose weight." And she was saying, "And if you really loved me, the weight would not matter that much to us and I would lose it." One's patience can be pressed beyond the breaking point, but there is some truth in what each is saying. It is almost as though they have set up the problem to see what the limits of acceptance are. Should the wife take the six-month reducing program alone? Should the husband grit his teeth and give her the talking-touching love she says she must have if she is to lose weight?

The problem goes much deeper. Acceptance has to do with the way we make each other *feel*. The wife did not feel accepted by her husband. She felt inadequate as wife, mother, and mate among his friends. Her laugh was loud and nervous. Her ideas faded quickly. Her feelings were unclear, her opinions equivocating, her gossip malicious. She was unsure of herself. He did nothing to reassure and support her, but merely let her hang there and get fat, and left her in her misery by blaming her extra twenty pounds for his rejection.

To build acceptance, it would be necessary for him to affirm his desire to be close to her by accepting the present weight condition, which he had helped to create, and moving close enough to her for her to put together a contract with him. The weight is just a symptom. He would need to say something like this: "I care about you. I have no need to hurt or neglect you. I want you to feel that I not only love you, but also I accept you as you are right now. I am glad you are in my world. I have the feeling that I sometimes make you feel insecure, and I want you to talk with me about those feelings, so together we can do something to change them. I want both of us to accept you."

Acceptance does not mean that, no matter what, I accept you and your condition. It is not a "your mate, love me or leave me" situation. It is not fair to ask that our mate simply tolerate whatever condition we present. Acceptance says: "I understand where you are, and I trust your goodwill to do something about the situation. I will support you in every healthy way possible while you work on the situation. Wherever I can help, I will. Trust me, and be sure to tell me how you need me."

Acceptance says that I am prepared to let you be who you are, and at the same time let you know (feedback) how you make me feel. I will do this as honestly and gently as I can. I trust you to be open to my feelings and help me to communicate to you in the most constructive way possible. Little things help. For example, tell me when I am too quick to criticize, when it is the wrong time or place, or when you feel that I am unfair. Trust the process. If each wants acceptance, yet each needs the mirror of the other, we must be honest and open, believing that we can both grow toward becoming the persons we want to be for ourselves and one another.

Again, in the religious world the need is to know that God knows and accepts his creatures. Paul Tillich, the great twentieth-century theologian, said that the heart of the Christian gospel is the message: "You are accepted." It is the longing of every human soul to experience a profound sense of being ultimately acceptable and unconditionally accepted. Even as children we want that from our parents: *not* "I will love you if you are good," but "I love you regardless."

Friendship requires a level of acceptance that encourages the dialogue forward, allowing a lifetime of devotion and celebration. Anxiety surrenders in the arms of acceptance.

The Need to Like and Be Liked

To know, trust, accept, and *like* another brings us to the first clear sign of love in our movement toward genuine intimacy in adult marriage.

To like someone is different from loving. To like means to take pleasure in, to enjoy, to feel good in another's presence. When apart, we feel the distance, miss the other, and desire reunion. When apart, by phone we say, "It is so good just to hear your voice." When we reunite, it may be, "Let me look at you."

Most friendships are *about* something: ideas, people, things, games, activities. Some people are just fun to be with. We seek them out, curious to find out what they are doing now. They amuse us, add zest. We like them. They seem to like us. "No big deal, no heavy agenda."

Somehow, it seems important in friendship to know where the action is with each other, where the energy is flowing, what has your best attention, where your life is focused. We have these kinds of friendships, and know what they are about, how they feed us. It is also a creative thing to do in marriage, to have exchanges in which we share the exciting centers of our lives as they keep emerging. This is not to displace other friendships. But a flat, dull friendship is an anomaly and can be disastrous to a healthy marriage. It is hard to *like* in a relationship that is a drag.

We usually like those who give us good feelings. We take delight in them. We want to be close to them. We feel comfortable with them. There is the lightness of humor and spoofing. A *guess what* spirit animates meetings: guess what I did, read, heard, saw. *Guess who* can be fun, if it does not degenerate into vicious gossip. We need to bring something to our meeting with friends. We bring ourselves, but that sounds a bit pretentious and abstract. People are also about something. The style, content, and feeling of sharing what we are about is what gets the "I really like being with you" sort of exchange flowing.

If the relationship is reciprocal, connections are created ("I'm glad you feel that way too"; "We seem to know a lot of the same people"; "Let's get together again some time soon"). Bonds are established ("You really make me feel good"; "I'm sure glad you are around today"; "I need to see you right away"). Expectations are exchanged ("I knew I could count on you"; "You were the first one I wanted to see"; "The nicest thing about London will be that you are there"). All of these feelings need not die in marriage. They are always available in all of us, with somebody, for somebody.

There are times when "I like you" carries even deeper feelings of that moment than if the person should say "I love you." There is a celebrative spirit, a *joie de vivre* in the enthusiastic "I like you" that confirms the moment and links the persons as little else does. The *liking* side of marriage is analogous to the resonance of a good violin. No matter how accurate the notes, the music does not get out; it does not go anywhere, unless the body of the instrument speaks. Married couples need to like each other. When you really think about it, why should people want to be married at all, if they do not like each other? Friendship is the most persistent thing about a great love, and probably the last thing to go in a great marriage, lasting "till death us do part." It is hard to imagine such friendship between people who do not truly love each other.

The Need to Share

I recall once leaving in the middle of a film because the woman I most wanted to share it with could not be there. It was a powerful, moving story, which at that time made me think of our relationship, and I could not handle the feelings the movie aroused in me. I knew I would need to discuss them with her, if she could not experience them with me. We returned to the movie together a week later, and I was glad I had waited.

Dian and I have found that writing letters to each other is often a good way to share. Some things are easier that way, both for the writer who wants to get it down just right, and the reader who may need to ponder those words by rereading before replying. Poems are often even more poignant and passionate, with feelings exposed and the heart vulnerable as at no other time. Also, I suggest you write it and share it for a response. Expect one, ask for one if you want. This is not your journal. It is a letter to a very special person and usually implies that a reply is desired.

Dear Dian:

Sharing with you is one of the most intimate experiences of my life. We have discussed almost everything so far. And I do not feel diminished, as some have told me they do. Rather, I feel clearer, stronger, richer. At first we were threatened by the things we each needed to say. So we shared our feelings about that, and I guess we decided that if we could not discuss the hard things, what *would* we be sharing in this marriage? No one is a fully disclosed person, but having you at the end of the day to share deeply in my life helps to keep the mystery of us alive, helps to make the magic of meeting a time to await and cherish. And when you open your day to me, I recall the moment as a little boy when I climbed a few feet into a great tree and peered for the first time into a blue-jay's nest of small greenish, speckled eggs. I am glad that we decided long ago to share with each other in a warm ritual of daily meeting every evening even when raising three children.

We have shared our gods, the men and women who have ennobled our lives with their ideas and creations: the philosopher and artist, musician and painter, parent and friend, teacher and mentor, the feeling and doing people who called us to be who we were at a time and place of revelation, when the path turned upward toward the mountain, downward into the valley, beside the clear stream, beyond the wall or to the sea. We have shared all. Or at least all that mattered. Also, we have hung back and waited for the other to emerge from dark encounters and said, "You made it. I knew you would. I could only wait." You were there. You are here. I am glad.

We have shared our dreams, the fantasies left over from childhood, the broad-scoped visions of how life might be fashioned, and the drab whims of our poverty or fatigue that fester out of the wouldn't-it-be-nice-if-once-before-we-die quarrels with life's knuckle sandwich. We have dreamed together: "Then what will we do?" We have pricked each other's bubble: "And if you got it, what would you do with it?" We have even demanded dreams when it seemed there were only nightmares: "You're a drag. Look around. There's water in Missouri. Let's buy a little sailboat. The roses are blooming in Loose Park. Write me a poem. If you want that degree, we'll find a way to get to Chicago . . . all five of us, all five of us."

We have shared our grief: our fathers, our mothers, all dead. We knew they really loved us, and so we celebrated them, even in their passing. The other tears: Korea, the tortured letters and the stupid, shortwave phone call from Tokyo, and Jenny, a year old before I saw her; the theological trip, Baptist and Unitarian ("What shall we teach our children?"), the joyous devotional watch we kept in Groton and Storrs, only to leave sightless from Seminary Hill, weeping through the prayer-poems; the late-night vigils with our three children needing to escape us into the world. And so much more. This is grief? Readers will complain that ours was nothing. But it was ours, and it got us in the gut. And who is to say among the mourners which heart is heaviest? You carry what you must, and if it is more than before, you may cry out among the saddest, and who will say it is nothing?

We have shared our guilt, nothing too heavy, mind you. No great schism of the soul or body. Just the little things: "Sex is celebration, not apology. It was my time with my son, and you stole it. You double your mileage with your gifts to me by bragging about them. Vacations with your folks are more work than play. It's only a car, dear. Would you please rethink your role as wife? Your house, my bills. There was nothing wrong with what you did, except that I felt abandoned at our own party." All of these a clutter of pique and selfishness, a brief loss of caring, a raw irritability, and just plain spite. So much for guilt. I never once meant to hurt you, nor you me. We always knew that guilt trips were such a waste. Straight-arrow friendships are rare, and even then seldom real. We do not offer cheap grace. We are still learning to forgive.

I love you!
Warren

The Need to Confront

Confrontation in friendship usually means that anger is aroused either before, during, or after the confrontation. It is important that the anger be dealt with as creatively as possible. The late Dr. David Mace, who wrote the foreword to the first edition of this book, gave us what I refer to as the three R's of responsible anger. He urged that we first *recognize* the anger for what it is and call it by name, just as soon as it arises. Second, we must be willing to *renounce* our right to vent it in fury, because fighting is not appropriate to a loving relationship. Finally, we should *request* help from our friend in exploring and dealing with the hurt feelings that triggered the anger.

Whatever our feelings as to what a creative use of anger is in the friendship of marriage, or however impossible it may seem to keep the peace, it must be agreed that anger is a healthy signal warning us of trouble in the relationship, while fighting is most often destructive and to be avoided. If the confrontation should come to rage and what can only be called a fight, it is important that these eruptions be flushed. When the life channels between friends get clogged with rage, it must be expelled in order to protect the integrity of relationships. Otherwise, the creative channels are polluted and the poisons of anger suffuse the entire human exchange. Anger in relationships is natural and might be seen as a waste product, even as the body creates other kinds of waste that must be flushed. Learning how to flush this anger will be one of the most creative things a couple can accomplish.

Blocking. It may be dangerous to your health and that of the relationship to refuse to pay attention to your anger, no matter how inappropriate the feeling may seem to you. My deceased friend and colleague Tom Green once mystified a client after the client's recitation of severe marriage problems previously undisclosed to anyone, when he asked if she also had problems with constipation. She admitted that she had been pestered by acute problems of that nature for years.

There are reasons why we block our anger. In some homes the expression of anger is forbidden on religious grounds (anger is sinful) or because a parent cannot emotionally cope with the upset. In other homes, one parent rages about and terrifies the others: anger becomes the enemy. If parents quarrel endlessly, children may decide that disagreements lead to arguments and grinding noises. Ugly words lead to violence. Anger is frightening. When children escape these homes, they may have trouble managing anger creatively.

When Allen was growing up, only his father was allowed to get angry. Mother whispered around the house, warning the children, "Now don't upset your daddy. You know how he gets." Out of this came an adult son who imitated his father with a terrible rage, breaking furniture and clearing bars with his bare fists. The skinny pale daughter was hurt and pouting most of the time and unable to discuss with her husband the things that angered her. Another son was a policeman who looked perfect, but was arrested for operating a huge, sophisticated burglary network.

Beth's parents had said, "Christians do not get angry." She and her sister were not allowed to yell at each other, much less scrap. Beth began to suffer migraine headaches at seventeen when her sister, thirteen months younger and looking very mature, "stole" Beth's boyfriend by promising sex. Beth was enraged but felt she could do nothing; she sat by and watched her sister come and go with her former boyfriend. As a wife, Beth was not better. The headaches persisted, and guilt blocked her expression of anger. When asked what she did with her anger, she said, "I pray." When asked about the headaches, she answered, "I take my medicine and go to bed, sometimes for two or three days." The headaches punished her, and going to bed punished her husband, whom she saw as selfish and untrustworthy.

Mary was from a suppressed German Lutheran family in Iowa. No feelings of any consequence were expressed. She could not recall being touched by her father, and her only clear recollection of her mother touching her was when she brushed her hair. This was usually a painful experience and unhappily associated with mother's hands. Mary's husband described her as cold, mousey, quiet, and not interested in sex. Her face was set, and her eyes seemed clouded over. Nothing ever really excited her, and she felt that life was meant to be endured, like intercourse. Their pastor had sent them to me after Mary's husband had asked for a divorce.

To block anger is probably one of the most physically damaging things a person can do with feelings. Anger is an energy that must go somewhere. We ignore it at our peril, because just when we think we have successfully suppressed it, we find that our body is complaining with aches and pains and perhaps severe illness or that we are taking the anger out on the wrong person.

We block by *denying* ("It's not important"); by *pretending* ("He didn't really mean it"); by *excusing* ("I probably would have done the same thing if I were in his shoes"); by *being a martyr* ("It's my fault"); and by *delaying* ("I'll let it go *this* time"). Behind these dams accumulate the enormous energy of anger, which may begin to contaminate the body systems of the person as well as the relational systems of the friendship. Under extreme circumstances, either or both may even die from it.

Discharging. Once a decision is made to acknowledge and own the anger, it is then possible to decide how best to discharge it. Here again, talking and touching may be necessary. Ideally, we should be able to tell our friend that we are angry and cause a discussion to come about in which the anger is dissolved. The key here is for our friend to take us seriously, accepting the fact that we are really and truly angry, regardless of how he or she feels about the anger—that is, whether it is justified, appropriate, or properly targeted on him or her. It is best when the anger is honored, so to speak, as something that we have a *right* to have. Only then can a healthy discussion follow as to what can best be done about it. Talking through is often a painful and frightening process. Consequently, we are tempted to avoid it, which can be even more dangerous.

Occasionally, even the talking is not enough. A person may be heard and accepted, but the accumulation of anger is just too great and cannot be expelled through talking. With me present, occasionally I have allowed couples to use a pillow to bang on the one who is the target, providing both agree to such an exercise. While both know it is a mock battle, they have been able to get anger out and transferred and even symbolically to "get back at" the other without engaging in some destructive behavior inappropriate to a successful resolution of the problem.

Dorothy said to Ted after he admitted to having an affair, "I'm furious with you. I could just shake you within an inch of your life. Why did you do such a thing to us?" No reason could be found except that the other woman was attractive and willing, and Ted was interested. Ted suggested Dorothy pound on him with a cushion for a few moments if it would make her feel better. He covered his head and she banged away. Ted did not feel humiliated and did not rise angry when Dorothy finally threw the cushion at him and said, "Get up, you bum." He peeked out, and got up looking somewhat chagrined. Dorothy, not a large woman, then slapped at him. He ducked, and she threw herself into his arms sobbing. After three or four minutes of crying, she stopped, blew her nose, and announced, "Okay, Stud, let's go home." In a few subsequent sessions we talked further about causes and results, and how such experiences might be avoided. The marriage had survived two years since their brief therapy and seemed healthy when I last spoke to them at a workshop.

Resolution. Anger is your friend in that it has signaled that you are unhappy. To deny the presence of anger is as foolish as denying the presence of fever. Getting the anger out to someone – the implicated party or another friend or counselor – permits the discharge of the distracting and disturbing energy. It may allow for a resolution of the problem and the reaffirmation of the relationship. While the precipitating event may be so destructive that discharging anger is not sufficient to dissolve the event, the person is emptied of hostile, damaging feelings, and both parties know the intensity of the pain, hurt, and ruin of the experience. This knowledge can be critical in dealing with guilt feelings, as well as equipping both to avoid precipitating events of alienation and disaffection in the future.

If the event is not fatal for the relationship, a resolution should come. Out of the fight emerges new *understanding*, the asking and giving of *forgiveness*, with a promise and *contract* to guard against that sort of thing in the marriage, or at least to be more alert and handle it more effectively if there is a next time.

The sequence, then, is something like this:

1. Get in touch with your feelings as quickly as possible after any signal of being disturbed.
2. What is the feeling? Name it. If it is anger, acknowledge it to yourself. Claim it. Own it.
3. Locate the source of the anger: who, when, where, how, and why, simply and clearly.
4. Address your friend, *privately* if possible, and from your *adult* self: "When you did (said) that, I felt angry toward you. I want to discuss it with you."
5. Insist that your anger be honored for discussion, even if your friend feels it is inappropriate.
6. Be fair. Hear his or her feedback. Search for an explanation that satisfies both parties, but do not explain away the feelings.

7. Get the feelings out. Talking should do it. If yelling occurs, remember that this can greatly alarm children and further inflame your feelings. Do a *ritual pounding* with a cushion only if both agree, and preferably in the presence of a therapist.
8. Ask and give forgiveness.
9. Contract to guard against recurrence.
10. Do something different. Take a walk or a bath together. Make love if you both want to. Reconnect.

The Need to Be Free

Friendships can become emotional traps. In marriage this is especially true. We begin to depend upon the safety and security of the relationship, especially if the trust level is good there and not so good everywhere else. Talking with the spouse can become comfortable, easy, and familiar. Behavior requires fewer explanations, and innovation is often neither wanted nor expected. We can be lazy, sloppy, conventional, even hackneyed and banal, and the spouse will excuse us and simply hope for better. It is important, then, that we pay attention to our need to be free, so that we do not become victims of an overindulging spouse or of our own resignation.

Free to Discover Self. We lay a lot of heavy expectations upon the married relationship. Some marriages suffer because people try to get almost all of life done there. With little privacy and much intimacy, all of the play, entertainment, work, and community are attempted within the context of marriage and its immediate environs. Such a marriage can become ingrown and dull. Even those who genuinely prefer it this way miss out on the feeding and challenge of people and experiences beyond the marriage. The mirror idea is important in marriage and family. We become mirrors for one another as we live in each other's presence; and with the verbal and nonverbal reflections (feedback) that we receive, we are able to see how we are doing as persons and family members. To have a friend in marriage over a period of years who is an accurate and reliable mirror is one of the greatest gifts of marriage. Still, others can assist in this feedback. Also, others may be more apt than the spouse to encourage us to move from mirrors to windows where we can look out to the moving, changing world that invites us to expand and grow.

Marriage should not inhibit the creative processes of the maturing adult to the degree that the person is diminished and unrealized. There are contractual limits that enable the marriage to thrive in trust and the individuals to enrich their lives, but limits must not make marriage a prison that generates resentment and bitterness.

Marriage must provide for *privacy*, which we shall discuss more fully in chapter 4. Privacy means that I must allow time and space for me, to include not only grooming but also those things that permit me to feel that I am an entity without appendages of other people and responsibilities. I need to feel that I have time and energy to take care of me: body, mind, and spirit. I may need time to read, think, reflect, write, paint, plant, or make something that says that *I am important; I respect my needs; I love me.* For it is only as I pay attention to my privacy that I am fit and able to move into relationship. A mother should not have to lock herself in her own bathroom just to have a little privacy and then have to be satisfied with the quality and quantity of it.

Jan had four young children. Her husband, Ev, was a lineman with the power company. There was not a lot of money, but there were no major problems regarding finances. Ev liked football and a little beer. He did not like housework or taking care of kids. When Jan collapsed from "nervous exhaustion," her physician referred them both to me. The major task was to help Jan make room for herself and get support for that program from Ev. We managed to get part of one day and one evening, which were hers to plan and use as she chose, with an allowance from the budget (Ev had one also) for "mad money." It made an enormous difference in her spirit and energy, as well as her attitude toward Ev and the children. The therapist toward whom he had been so hostile suddenly became his friend. "She's a different woman," he said. "Everybody's feeling better, even the baby." And it wasn't just a matter of giving Ev's servant a little time off. He became a supportive friend in the new patterns, getting supper, bathing children, and baby-sitting on her night off, as well as paying more attention to ways of helping at home, and relieving her of all of the directing, managing, and disciplining processes of the family. On her half-days she shopped, visited, or bowled with a friend. Some nights she just went over to her aunt's house, had soup and a sandwich with her, watched TV, and played one game of Chinese checkers. Jan laughed when she told me, and she said, "I know you think that's dumb, but I actually had fun." Ev played poker one night a week and got into some difficulty with his buddies when their wives found out about "Jan's freedom."

A marriage should be strong enough to permit people to move out of each other's circle of expectations occasionally without the other feeling rejected or abandoned. A person should feel free to say, "We always watch this program, but I will read for a while and go to bed early tonight." Even promises to visit friends or relatives or to take in a movie should be open to recontracting when you need to do something for yourself which has a kind of urgency about it. The freedom to be alone within the demands for intimacy must be assured if autonomy is to be preserved and the person is to be nurtured.

Free to Cultivate Primary Relationships. Marriage is an *exclusive* relationship. There is no other experience like it. We have expectations, make commitments, and satisfy needs uniquely in marriage. The law permits only one husband or wife at a time. If a man and a woman are husband and wife, each is unique to the other, and the legal bond is exclusive.

From that legality flows any number of commitments that are exclusive to the marriage: the absolute exclusivity of their child's parentage; joint ownership of property; certain traditional public behavior such as living together; private understandings; and the intimate promises of husband and wife. A marriage will hardly simultaneously tolerate another look-alike.

Monogamy has not fared well in our so-called free society, even though women are more and more autonomous. Certainly polygamy would not survive in a society of liberated women. Some argue for multiple mates for both husband and wife in marriage. The human being is remarkably adaptable. However, I am better convinced that a man and a woman entering self-consciously into an exclusive relationship and creating their marriage out of the incredible uniqueness of themselves can experience something extraordinary: the immense possibility of each self, and each-in-union in the circle of intimacy. Marriage should also support each person's friendships among members of the same sex. Men and women relate in their same-sex, primary relationships in ways that are critical to emotional health. Something gets done there that seldom happens in any other relationships with mate, family, children, parents, or friends of the opposite sex. Topic, vocabulary, and style can shift dramatically with a same-sex, close friend. Some women still call it *girl talk*, even though they are apt to get the heavy-lidded condescending smile from those who see such women as unliberated.

Among men, it is referred to as *male bonding*, even though that sounds silly and pretentious to most of us, like a category invented for someone's research grant. Whatever we call it among males or females, we need to check out how we are doing among our own sex, exchange the *in* talk, swap "helpful hints," spoof the opposite sex, and in countless ways exorcise the demons that mates plant in us. The gang is a sanctuary, a haven, and a retreat for some. For others, it is a brief respite. For all of us, it is a place to affirm ourselves and enjoy.

George and his father bred and sold dogs. They spent much time going to dog shows, and discussing their own animals on the phone. Otherwise they saw each other only on family occasions. George was not dependent on his father, and his father was not controlling. Cile, George's wife, was jealous, saying it was unnatural for a grown son to spend so much time with his father. George was angry and hurt. He liked his father and was glad they were friends. Cile was not interested in dogs, turning up her nose at "those stinking animals." For five years the dog question created a crisis in the marriage that took almost six months to resolve. Cile never learned to share George's hobby, but she did come to respect the relationship he had with his father when she better understood how angry she was toward her own father, who had rather cruelly rejected her.

Healthy marriages can permit primary relationships with members of the opposite sex. Many couples will feel this is the most dangerous freedom of all. We may avoid it in deference to the mate's uneasiness, or because we ourselves fear losing control of our emotions. *What if . . .* hovers about the most innocent relationship with a member of the opposite sex. *Be careful*

... guards interesting relationships of emerging closeness. *Hide it* ... may shadow relationships that are clearly exciting, which signals *hide it* from the other person, yourself, or your mate.

One would think it unnecessary, but my work with married couples seems to require that we say here that a healthy marriage might allow for simple exchanges of affection, deep conversation, and innocent meetings between men and women who are not married to each other. The complaints I hear are from people who resent the mate greeting a person of the opposite sex with a hug, having a long, serious conversation with him or her at a party, or going to lunch with that person. I have yet to find a single instance of such behavior that was not safe, if not totally innocent. Most people who are going to "play around" are usually careful *not* to hug, kiss, touch, talk, or go to lunch so openly. I assume there are those who try to cover an affair with this byplay as a smoke screen, but most of us are not clever enough to hide the innuendo and subtle signals. Better to play it cool and keep the friendship that way. Those who touch and talk as expressions of genuine affection outside the marriage are sincere about those communications and would defend them even to a suspicious mate.

Two problems are usually posed. One is the domino theory which says that it is better not to get too friendly. This is like the teetotaler who says that a person would never become an alcoholic if that first drink were never taken. That is not an accurate cause-and-effect description of what creates an alcoholic. Nor does a hug, quick kiss of greeting, long talk, or lunch mean that we have the beginnings of an affair. We might, but the affair would not happen unless a lot of other things were going on in both lives and in the marriage that contributed to such an alliance. If a marriage is not strong enough to risk these simple communications of friendship, it needs attention.

The second problem has to do with people having to give up friends of the opposite sex just because they get married. The arguments are: most of those were romantic relationships (which is usually not true of *most* of them) and are better off retired; or the person should become the friend of both the husband and wife, which is often difficult to manage; or, the anxious mate will say, "I'm prepared to give up my old friends for you. Why can't you do the same for me?" For this person that usually means that friends are easily discarded, or there is great anxiety about the possibility of extramarital relationships.

Actually, the primary, legitimate complaint from a mate in this matter usually has to do with one of them feeling embarrassed and neglected while the other gives attention to the friend. However, there are many marriages in which the couple know and experience each other's love even as both maintain warm relationships with friends of the opposite sex. I think this can be an important sign of a healthy, adult marriage, and can even prove enriching.

Finally, the ultimate freedom in friendship is the freedom to leave. In *Spheres of Intimacy*, my sequel to the earlier edition of this book, I tell a story from my practice that best illustrates this aspect of freedom, and deserves repeating here. A couple came to see me for marriage counseling soon after I met them in a workshop. Even before she sat down the wife said, "Now, Dr. Molton, you need to know that regardless of what happens in these sessions, I will never leave this man." I looked at him and he winked. For a split second I debated acknowledging his response, then asked, "Did you see that?" She asked, "See what?" And I answered, "When you said you would never leave him, he winked." Surprised, she said, "So?" I paused, hoping they might better catch the point, and said, "You just gave away all your power." A marriage must not always be up for grabs, but it should never be without the honesty of critique, even to the point of the ultimate question: Can this marriage survive *any* behavior? I do not believe a relationship of integrity should be "promised away" under any circumstances. We must know that each is free to go, or else there is no accountability. I doubt that believing our mate would never leave, regardless of our behavior, would help either partner to create a great love. Such a decision sounds more like a set-up for catastrophe than the formula of commitment, more like dependency than devotion.

Chapter 4

PARTNERS: MARRIAGE AS COVENANT AND CONTRACT

Along with its religious and cultural sentiments, marriage may also be seen as a small corporation, a business union of partners who have contracted to meet each other's needs. Such a view in no way diminishes the social, aesthetic, religious, and personal values of marriage. Rather, it may help focus on the bonds and business of the relationship.

Let us consider two basic concepts: *covenant* and *contract*. Covenant is at the heart of the Hebrew-Christian tradition and dominates its literature. The oldest body of Hebrew law is called *The Book of the Covenant*. God had a personal covenant with Abraham and later through Moses with Israel in *The Sinaitic Covenant*. Israel was to obey God's law in exchange for his grace. It was a comprehensive, life-embracing plan that suggests the intimacy of lovers: husband and wife, as in the book of Hosea.

Covenant ideas are also present in Christianity. Jesus is seen as being the new covenant promise of God. Jesus appeared as the love covenant, fulfilling the law covenant that was binding upon his followers. There is the metaphor of Jesus as Bridegroom and his church as Bride.

Hence, the concept of covenant is woven into the fabric of our culture. It carries in it deep implications for integrity and commitment. Rising out of the heart of our two major religious faiths, covenant is the ultimate bonding of lovers. It is a signal to the world of interdependency welded in alliance.

Marriage as *covenant* is a relationship in which husband and wife commit themselves to each other in a *quid pro quo* arrangement, promising faithfully to respond to each other's needs and gifts. The covenant says: *I want to do life with you.* It is a broad and deep commitment, a bond of pairing and joining. So long as both are sworn, the trust is inviolable.

The *contract* is different. It is less permanent, a rule of the game, which can be renegotiated at any time and simply tells us how it is between us just now. The covenant says: *I want to do life with you.* The contract says: *And here is how, now.*

Some years ago a young man announced in my office that his wife had lied to him. When they married she promised to be wife and mother, and now she wanted to return to nursing, which she had abandoned soon after their wedding when she became pregnant. I asked him where he worked and he said, "Ford Motor Company, on the line."

"How do you like it?" I asked.

"Great," he said. "Been there twelve years."

"Good money?" I asked.

"You bet," he said. "Enough for both of us and two boys to get along just fine. But now she thinks it's not good enough."

His wife protested but he kept talking. "My mother raised four boys and she never worked a day in her life." He, of course, meant "outside the home." His wife and I exchanged glances.

Then I said that it sounded like he was married to the Ford Motor Company. He saw the humor and we all laughed nervously. "You could say that," he added.

"Ever get a new contract since you've been with Ford?" I asked.

"Oh sure, we do a new contract every couple of years. . . ." His voice trailed off and he said with a grin, "You rascal!"

"That's all your wife wants," I offered. "She loves the covenant. She just wants to update the contract." And I proceeded to explain the difference.

It is important to use these two words to differentiate between the promise and bond as contrasted with rules and arrangements. Couples would not be so alarmed if they would use covenant and contract differently. Only the death of the relationship dissolves the covenant. Mutual agreement renegotiates contracts, which are the working tools of the marriage. Marriage is covenant. The *business* of marriage is done by the ever-changing contracts, which may be simple understandings or hard-fought agreements arrived at after deep searching and hard work on both sides. It is easy to see that it is in the partnership idea of marriage that the ability to negotiate needs becomes critical. The skills of dialogue, the management of feelings, proper perceptions of reality, a gift for compromise, and the ability to keep one's word are the tools of negotiation. Contracting in marriage is an art that must be continually practiced and refined.

Eva and Ralph came for counseling after five years of marriage, when it became clear that Eva, at twenty-eight, required a complete hysterectomy. Ralph was depressed, suppressing anger and disappointment. Eva was the youngest of three girls, and her oldest sister had been adopted. She was sad about her loss, but thought they could adopt children. Ralph was an only child of successful parents, who had considerable ego investment in their son, an attorney as was his father. His parents had never approved of Eva and used the news of her hysterectomy to ask some disturbing questions. His mother even said, "I would think, Ralph, that it would be impossible for you to love someone who could not honor your manhood with a child."

In the first session Ralph was quiet. Eva talked, weeping softly now and then, as Ralph cautiously patted her hand. When asked what he was feeling, he said, "Sad, sad for her. It's a great disappointment, you know. She really wanted children." To a further question he said, "Oh, sure. I had my heart set on fathering my own child." They had spoken briefly about adoption, but he was clearly suffering from the loss of a chance to father a child.

Later I spoke alone with Ralph. He was not happy about the thought or prospects of adoption. Babies were not plentiful. But there was something more. "Maybe I want out of this marriage. She is half a woman. I am a whole man. I don't want to raise just any child. I want to see *my* wife carrying *my* child, from *my* sperm. Is that too much for a man to ask? Hell, if I had known this would happen, I doubt I would have married her." He was angry, his voice in a strong stage whisper. I waited. He was pensive. His eyes filled. Then he looked at me and said, "How the hell do you tell a woman *that*? Only an S.O.B. would leave her now."

The covenant had been: I want to do my life with you. The understood contract had been: and there shall be children. The contract could not be honored and would require renegotiation. The covenant was threatened, but it could not automatically be disregarded. Ralph still seemed to want his marriage. We went on from there.

Eva was afraid Ralph would leave her. "He adores kids, and there is such family pride, especially on his father's side, what with Ralph's three uncles and all their kids. Ralph is an only child, and his folks always want the best from him. Now look."

"At what?" I asked.

"At me. I've ruined everything. If I were half a woman . . ." she paused, shocked at her own pun. "If I had any guts, I'd offer him a divorce."

"But what about adoption?" I asked.

"I'm afraid to talk about it any more. He does not want just any kids. He wants *his*. Besides, I really think his folks would reject an adopted child." She felt helpless.

In all our sessions both Ralph and Eva expressed anger and fear as we tried to sort out the contract options, never accepting the idea that the covenant was in jeopardy.

Further sessions enabled us to examine all the gifts and promises of their covenant. Ralph became more autonomous regarding his parents and more supportive toward Eva. They found ways to enhance the marriage and spent more time doing the things they enjoyed early in their relationship. They quit agonizing over the child question. They confronted his parents with their rejection of Eva. They reaffirmed their marriage to his parents, who visibly warmed toward Eva. The marriage deepened and expanded. Eva began night courses toward her master's degree in elementary education. They entertained more, played more, took long weekends out of town, and moved to a condominium on a lake where they could sail. With their friendship nurtured, their love life became "fun, even funny sometimes," as Eva described it, "and for the first time, not so serious as before."

Then, after about six months of weekly sessions, Eva called me early one morning to say that Ralph had asked that they talk again about initiating adoption procedures, and for that he wanted them to take a long weekend away. As she canceled the appointment for Saturday, she said quietly, "I feel so loved." It was working out. Six years later the marriage was alive and well, with Mark and Daphne added to the family.

A part of the process in this marriage crisis was to strengthen the covenant (I want to do life with you) when the contract regarding children threatened to destroy the marriage. The love and friendship were enhanced, so that the contract could be renegotiated. Once it was again clearly established that they wanted to do life together, the petty quarrels were seen for what they were and ignored the second time around. Love was needing children, rather than the ego needing affirmation. Children in that family could then experience the most important factor in their own emotional health: *parents who love each other.*

Partners do the business of marriage. There is a legal document called a marriage license. They jointly hold property, enter into contracts with utilities and business firms, earn and administer sums of money, parent children, and often become owners of business enterprises.

If we are to understand something of the contractual aspects of the business of marriage, we must examine the process of partnership. Contracting in marriage is a daily business: Who will pick up the children? How shall we spend the evening? When shall we plan the vacation? Who will get the next new car? The items change; the dynamics shift; but there are a few basic concepts that remain fairly constant in the process of making a partnership work, and in that process some basic needs be get met.

Equality

In a marriage of autonomous adults, it is important for partners to feel like equals, sharing mutually in the rewards or losses of the partnership. This has to do with respect. A man, having an affair with a woman while he was still married, said after some reflection, "Even if I get a divorce, I wouldn't marry her. I don't respect her. She isn't my equal. Does that mean I'm a snob?"

He was not a sexist or an elitist. She was not his peer, not in education, intelligence, interests, or values. It had nothing to do with snobbery. It was an honest recognition of critical differences. They were lovers of sorts but could not be partners. They would not have created an adult marriage.

In recent years we have heard a lot about equality. In the past there has been a trade-off of security for sex between men and women. Mutuality has begun to grow as women have discovered sex for themselves and learned to make money in jobs and professions that did not reduce them to role, function, or sex. There are many forms of prostitution. There is the old saw: "Every woman has her price, and for some it's marriage." Some women have felt prostituted in marriage. Sex was not for pleasure, but the product by which they bought for themselves financial security and respectability. Many women who work and earn wages feel more like equals with men as they negotiate relationships. Even if women quit work to stay home after marriage or the birth of the first child, there is still a new confidence and feeling of personal security. For years, I have had women report that they could not leave a bad marriage because they could not manage financially without a husband. Those who were determined managed to get out any way. However, it was true that to get a divorce would often have done violence to the lifestyle and opportunities of the family, much of which was critical to the health and welfare of the children. In theory it is easy to say, "An unhealthy marriage also does violence to a family." The notion of "Something is better than nothing" conditions the will, and a woman who feels helpless about earning her way will often stay where she is. It is mandatory that feelings of equality be mutually shared by men and women.

This is also true of sex. As women have more recently become better able to appreciate their sexuality and their right to pleasure, they have been less willing to "trade it off" for security in a bad marriage. They are less willing merely to "permit and endure" intercourse when they no longer care for the man. More reliable birth control has also enhanced a woman's autonomy.

Since money is the ticket to almost anywhere in our society, and the man traditionally has earned the family income, he has assumed a certain power and prestige that reinforced his feelings of superiority and the woman's of inferiority (of being spayed as the female counterpart to male castration by poverty) simply by virtue of his earning power. He often adds insult to injury by radically controlling his money or by refusing to allow his wife to work and earn her own money. He resorts to the tired cliches of what his mother did, or the jungle nature of the business world, the lecherous character of other men, his own exhaustion and need for his wife as "Mom," while at the same time implying that "woman's work" is easy and her freedom permits leisure, sunbaths, TV soap operas, and a generally casual life. Most women are enraged by these insults.

Mutual respect in partnership is not rooted in role, function, or sex. It is not determined by societal assignments for husband and wife, notions about man's work and woman's work, or the stereotypes of "Men are that way," or "That's just like a woman." It has to do with the ability to have a unique appreciation for the partner as a person with his or her personal gifts and needs. When our partner sees us uniquely, we feel esteemed and respected. It is this balanced, mutual respect that enables equality in the marriage. If I see my partner as inferior, I will not treat her as an equal. I will not adequately respect her. While unequals may be partners in certain enterprises, a healthy marriage demands equality.

Our best research today indicates that perhaps more than ever before young people are tending to marry peers. Now, if we can enable them to escape the stereotypes of role, function, and sex that tend to support notions of inequality, perhaps men and women can begin to treat each other fairly and reciprocally. There are some marvelous differences between men and women, but there is nothing that dictates feelings of inequality of persons so that either is exploited or abused.

In recent years the sexual and the economic revolutions have given women more options and hence greater power to negotiate their own destiny. As men have participated in these changes, we have gained greater autonomy along with the women. We have been relieved of our phoney macho roles that were so enslaving to both sexes and have shared creatively in all the ways that enable men and women to feel like peers. Sex for security is no longer a formula for marriage. Now partners assume that both will be working for good sex and real security for themselves and each other. This change alone represents an enormous shift toward equality in marriage.

Commitment

In the business of marriage, it is the task of partnership to ensure commitment. A friend may excuse himself. A lover is subject to moods. A partner is in the harness with you, pledged and present. The solo qualities of friend, partner, and lover are obvious. While distinct, they finally merge. However, I occasionally see a marriage saved – one that deserved saving – because one mate was genuinely committed to the partnership, even when the friend and lover dimensions of the marriage were in trouble.

A man had a superficial friendship with his wife and was in fact committed to his work. He had trouble finding love feelings for her and considered divorce. Only his pledge at the time of the wedding made him try. Then his wife had a serious auto accident. During her recovery he came to love and enjoy her again. Years later, just after his funeral, his wife said, "He wanted to leave me when the children were young. He stayed because of his promise. After my accident, we seemed to fall in love again." Their marriage lasted forty-two years. There may be many "if's" and "maybe's" in this woman's love story, but when I consider what might have been lost without the pledge or partnership, I know there is value in a healthy concept of unconditional commitment: "Come hell or high water, we are partners. What happens to you, happens to me."

If love turns to hate and friends become enemies, "partner" is meaningless and destructive, but often it is the one aspect that keeps people trying when it is hard to be friend or lover. It is more healthy for adults to work on the marriage because of their solemn pledge of partnership than, for example, to "stay in it because of the children." That puts the burden on the children, who have so much to gain by a good marriage between their parents and so much to lose by a bad one. Unhappy mates then often turn to the children to justify staying in the marriage. They turn to them for love, achievement, obedience, and approval, with the parents often in open competition for their children's affection. How much better for adults to explore the strength of their word *not to quit* in the face of weak friendship and pale love.

It is in the idea of partner that we cement the relationship against the whims and vagaries of friends and lovers. It is here that the agreement between adults is finally tested for sheer determination, grit, and stamina.

If there is one general criticism that might be leveled against today's divorcing couples, it is that despite the increased effort of marriage counseling, *many couples give up too soon* and after too little effort. Better grounding in the partnership aspect of marriage might help people hold on and work. Someone asked Winston Churchill why the English bulldog had such a flat nose, and he said, "So it can breathe without letting go." If there is some genuine commitment to being partners, a marriage may breathe without the couple letting go.

It is easy, here, to become emotionally trapped in a my-marriage-right-or-wrong loyalty to a relationship that has little to commend it. My plea is not for some sort of heroic fealty to a marriage that is little more than a piece of paper, nor is the partnership concept only the knot at the end of the rope or the arm-twister for *just in case*. The loyalty aspect of partner is rooted in the command function of oath: "You have my word that I will work on this marriage. Even if friend and lover are badly strained, I am still your partner, and between partners the word is *work*."

Negotiating Goals

Part of the work of partnership is negotiating compatibility between two autonomous adults. Strong people have strong opinions. Their feelings may run high. They call for action and each may want to command. Their values may not always mesh.

The task is to put together a third entity: their *compromise*. This is a key word in partnership. Compromise means to promise *together*. Working partners, then, submit their own will to the harmonized wills of both and, in such a blend of the best of each, find the action model that may meet the needs of the partnership. A somewhat idealized analogy of the spirit of compromise between equals is the twenty-four chromosomes that each parent contributes in the conception of another human being. Each partner makes his or her limited gift to the creation of a third entity, a person who will not be exactly like either.

There are many ways to organize the process by which partners and families accomplish goals. Following are eleven aspects of this process, illustrated by what my partner, Dian, and I put together for our family when it became clear that I wanted to enter a doctoral program.

1. Setting Goals. These often emerge from everyday living. Personal needs, accidents, a challenge in the environment, even a revelatory moment as in a dream may cause one or both partners to focus on a goal that requires negotiation, special planning, and extra resources. Once, for us, a goal was focused when, on a New Year's Day, Dian and I each made two lists for the coming year: "What I want for me" and "What I want for you." Then we exchanged them and discussed the possibilities. Another time, a special anniversary challenged us to plan and save for a trip to England.

Some years ago after many conversations, it became clear to us that I should shift my career as a seminary professor to include counseling in a clinical practice. We also thought our family might profit from the inner-city experience of a great metropolitan center. Our lifestyle and financial needs with three children moving toward college also made it imperative that both of us complete our graduate degrees. We had always talked together in the late evenings, and those times began to be consumed by these three goals.

2. Establishing Priorities. Goals pile up. Some are more important than others. Some are clearly feasible, others only marginally so. Some are short-term, while others will take time. Some are foundation and others are superstructure; they build on each other.

I needed and wanted a doctorate. Dian needed her master's degree if she were to command the position that could carry a major part of the family budget during my graduate program. Stephen, age sixteen, was near completion of high school. It might be possible for both him and me to enter schools in the same area, and he could live with us in order to reduce expenses. Jennifer, thirteen, and David, eleven, were excited about the move.

3. *Developing Alternatives.* One of the greatest causes for pain in the partnership is a win/lose mentality. What is needed is a *win/alternative* process, so that if the top priority is impossible, the partnership does not give up in despair. If you feel like a loser, it may be because you are setting yourself up with a formidable goal that has little chance of success, with the only alternative being loss and defeat.

Our first choice was the professional doctorate program at Chicago Theological Seminary, with my study including clinical work and a research fellowship at the University of Chicago Hospitals. If this were denied, we would try elsewhere. Other schools were investigated. Even if I were accepted, there might be housing problems or difficulty with Dian finding just the right teaching position. We considered, in that eventuality, my commuting once a month to our home in Kansas City. If Steve could not complete high school early, he would remain behind with friends. If he did graduate, we would try to get him in the Chicago Art Institute and the University of Chicago. If that failed, he would go to the state university.

4. *Assigning Tasks.* This phase usually has to do with gathering data, saving money, and investigating. It is what is referred to in business as a *feasibility study* and has primarily to do with preparation that will give clues as to the possibility of winning the goal.

I had to get myself accepted into the program. Dian would need to complete her master's degree. Steve had to accelerate his high school program by adding courses and attending summer school. Housing for the family and a job for Dian had to be found. Everybody got busy.

5. *Checking Risks.* Important goals often involve heavy risks. These must be openly and honestly faced, so that adequate defenses may be organized for protection and also in order that these might not be used as excuses to fail.

One risk for the family would be moving to Hyde Park in Chicago, an island in one of the world's most troubled ghettos. The impact of the culture shock upon the children was threatening. The financial security of the family was a concern. Then there was always the possibility of academic problems causing the program to be lengthened beyond the family's endurance. We knew the risks and discussed defenses against them. Our plans rolled on.

6. *Making Decisions.* Decisions were made through family conferences, letters, survey trips, phone calls, and interviews. The family was in accord on both our priorities and alternatives. Each one felt that his or her personal needs were being taken seriously and met. We mobilized our resources for a major educational experience for all of us.

When I was accepted into the program, the final decision to attend had to be made. It was decided that Dian would attempt to complete her M.A. during the summer while I began my work in Chicago. Steve agreed to forfeit his summer plans in order to attend summer school, as well as earn as much money as possible teaching art at a church in the ghetto. He would also apply for admission to the Art Institute of Chicago. A decision was made for the family to join me in Chicago in September. Dian would apply for teaching jobs in Chicago, and we would investigate housing once she found her school.

7. *Taking Action.* After all the planning and arranging, all the interviews, calls, letters, budgets, and loans; after all the careful blueprint and construction, there comes that magic moment when all systems are go and our show is on the road. It is the moment of ignition – a last phone call, an airplane send-off, packing the moving truck, and the early morning exit – something that says, "Now!"

Our lift-off came with my leaving for Chicago in June with our tired, old station wagon, which we could easily risk parking on the streets of Chicago (we had nightmare fantasies of car cannibalism). Dian and Steve entered summer programs in Kansas City. Dian received her M.A. degree on the hot, sad day of Robert Kennedy's funeral. Steve finished high school a year early and was admitted to the Art Institute of Chicago, the youngest student there. Dian was hired by Harvard-St.George, a private school in Chicago which Jenny and Dave would also attend. We found an apartment only a few blocks from the university and Harvard-St. George in a community of other graduate students in my program. In August I returned to Kansas City to move the family to Chicago in a rented van. Our first drive down Lake Shore Drive into the city was beautiful. We were excited. We were days away from the Democratic National Convention. A mood of foreboding was building in Chicago. But life seemed good. Our plan was working. We were not apprehensive. Taking action felt good.

8. Carrying Through. Carrying through means not running out of gas, crashing, or having to declare financial or emotional bankruptcy. It means keeping the plan alive, responsive to the dynamics of daily change and realistic adjustment to what will work toward the ultimate goal.

The Chicago sojourn was tough. There were many difficult times: struggles in the neighborhood, money concerns, academic stress, children under pressure, and the constant feeling of having to adapt to a sort of "camping out" lifestyle. We had family conferences, shared at least two meals a day, attended church on Sunday, and sought out the fascinating shops, museums, galleries, theaters, parks, dunes, and beaches in and around the Windy City. We ice-skated on the mall and swam at the pool of the university. We made new friends and did our share of the entertaining. Steve was robbed at knife point and lost a precious forty dollars earned at a tough job acting in a street theater cast in ghetto performances. I put together a book of poems called *Bruised Reeds*, and a new friend, David Breed, did the photographs. It was published the next spring. Steve liked the Art Institute, and Dian, Jenny, and Dave had a good year at Harvard-St. George. My doctoral program was exciting and demanding. There was good dialogue between my peer group and our professors, who were extraordinarily open to new ideas and processes in education and psychology, both of which seemed up for grabs in those days. My clinical work and research fellowship at the University of Chicago Hospitals were most challenging, and I especially appreciated taking a seminar with Elisabeth Kubler-Ross on death and dying when she was just beginning her research interviews with terminally ill patients and the medical teams. Our family was more than surviving; we were flourishing.

9. Doing Evaluation. Checkups occur along the way. Periodic inventories of "What's finished?" and "What's left?" are constantly falling away and rising in one's mind. Check lists, revised budgets, refrigerator notes, a new book, and special counsel for new input – all may contribute to the ongoing process of evaluation. At the end, when it is over, a more formal critique may be helpful, especially if the IRS is interested or still further programs are to emerge out of this one.

The process may be totally informal with a simple, "Well, we won't try that again," or "Wasn't that a great experience!" This is the most neglected part of any venture, and it would be the most valuable for the future. I once counseled with a man who was fifty-three years old, had failed three times in his field, and had twice declared bankruptcy. A critique somewhere along the way might have been helpful.

However, for those of us who overdo analysis, critique, and evaluation, I would call to mind Viktor Frankl's injunction in his book *The Unconscious God*, when he reminds us that the hunter's boomerang returns to him only when it has failed to hit the target. We turn back upon ourselves in prolonged reflection and diagnosis only when there is not something better to do that we do well. For this reason I felt it important to add goal number 11 to this process, "Returning to 'Go.' " Evaluation is mandatory, but it must not become an end in itself. A man once said at a meeting, "It seems to me we spend most of our time revising bylaws. What else are we supposed to be doing?" Right action is the best message to the ego.

For us, evaluation occurred on many occasions, from our chats with one another "about things," to family conferences, to grades, report cards, and bank balances. A new look at calculation and calendaring occurred when we missed Dian's birthday. We knew the *date* but somehow had confused the *day*, which we had all projected as Thursday, and it should have been Wednesday. Birthdays are big at our house; so by ten o'clock on Wednesday evening when nothing like a celebration had happened, Dian was upset, to say the least. We celebrated the next day as planned, while signs also went up around the apartment reading, "Remember! Next year December 4 really does fall on Thursday."

Like so many other things in life and relationships, in any significant project we have to *keep checking it out.*

10. Celebration or Commiseration. The outcome of the program means either a party or a wake. It is important to pay attention to the grief process if a major goal is lost. We hurt at those times. There is disappointment, perhaps even a deep sense of defeat and personal failure. There must be guards against depression and bitterness. Occasionally, it may even be helpful to talk it through with a trusted friend, counselor, or minister.

If the program is a success, everyone involved should find a way to celebrate. Unfortunately, we tend not to celebrate our own little personal victories – promotions, completion of school project, a new job, paying off a mortgage, or some other success. Birthdays or other important anniversaries deserve celebration and are excellent occasions for building a feeling of family or community.

There were parties in Chicago with other graduate students, their families, and later with old friends in Kansas City who had awaited our return. The program was a success in every way. We had even survived the truck-and-trailer exodus through the Chicago labyrinth when part of our caravan was lost and stranded. The family still celebrates as the children, older now, report things that continue to float to the surface and seem now all right to share with parents, some of which I am just as glad they sheltered me from at the time. The slides and home movies are celebrations, and we all keep asking for a showing on holidays.

11. Returning to "Go." After it is all over, it is time to move on. A failure in the primary goal means commitment to the alternative. Success calls for moving to the next phase, and restructuring.

For us, it meant Dian finding a teaching position in Kansas City. I returned to the seminary faculty and immediately also entered private practice as a pastoral counselor, doing therapy for individuals and couples. Steve transferred his study program to another college. Jenny and Dave were glad to be back home with friends, even though all had changed a lot.

A new and exciting project faced us: moving from seminary faculty housing to our own home. Return to "go"!

Dian and I have faced other vocational challenges which tested our marriage and seemed to leave our relationship stronger. My leaving full-time seminary teaching for private practice was for me like a divorce, since I had for twenty years been "married" to the church as pastor, chaplain, and professor

of pastoral counseling. Clinical practice took me further away
from the daily life of the church than I had ever been. As a minister's wife, Dian felt enormous changes taking place in her life
when I made this move, and we had to talk through these
changes until she felt reconciled.

In 1980 Dian's work in public television took her to Denver,
where she became vice-president in charge of educational ser-
vices for twenty-three stations in a dozen western states. For
two and a half years we had a commuter marriage every other
weekend between Denver and Kansas City or whatever city she
happened to be in. A whole series of challenges began to arise as
our family escorted Dian to Denver and moved her into her elev-
enth floor apartment overlooking the Rocky Mountain range
from Long's Peak to Pike's Peak. The successes and stresses of
that adventure continued to the week of her return, when she
arrived home just days before the tragic death of my dear friend
and business partner, Dr. Tom Green. She came home as my
other partner "returned home," as my hospice friend put it.

While Dian was in Denver she began her own personal Jungian analysis, a process developed by the great Swiss psychiatrist, Carl Jung, whose work she had come to appreciate during
a seminar which we attended together in Zurich in 1976. When
she returned to Kansas City from Denver, she decided she
wanted to begin training to become a Jungian psychotherapist,
for which she would also need a clinical degree. This required
her returning to graduate school for yet another master's degree, this time in social work, plus two major licensing exams
and her continuing personal psychoanalysis and Jungian semi-
nars. Needless to say this meant additional realignments in our
relationship to accommodate her vocational needs.

All of this is simply to remind us that marriage covenants require new contracts as life goals continue to change during the
course of the relationship. A major test of a marriage is how
well it adapts to these challenges. The bottom line of covenant
is: *Can I be me with you?* The dynamic tension between autonomy and intimacy persists in a healthy relationship.

Supporting Personal Life Goals

I hope it is now clear that one of the most important tasks of
the corporation is to help all members realize their personal life

goals. More and more frequently in marriage counseling I find that young couples are conflicted over personal goals. Yet there is a sense in which personal investment focuses differently in one's profession or avocation. A couple fought when the husband decided he wanted to leave general medical practice and prepare for psychiatry. The wife did not see "why he had to do that" when it was so expensive in time and money after their years of sacrifice. A man was greatly annoyed with the upset to the household when his wife's knitting for fun turned into knitting for profit, as she began to take orders for garments, rent looms, and start her own shop. Personal goals may cause inconvenience and distress, leaving formidable blocks in the path of the partnership.

One way to approach discussion of life goals is to delineate four major divisions of the human experience: *privacy, intimacy, community,* and *transcendence.* These are obvious categories, and the infinite possibility of description defies neat definition. A target construct may help us to see how interrelated they are, how each grows from the other, and how transcendence embraces it all. A cylinder of layers would add a third dimension. A sphere would offer still greater possibilities of energy and motion.

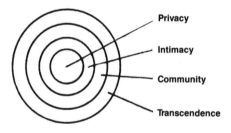

Let us now look at these circles separately.

Privacy

One's private world is the sphere of unique need and aspiration. It includes aloneness but is a richer and more complex dimension than simple solitude or the sense of being alone even in the presence of others. Privacy is me in that inimitable drama of me experiencing *me experiencing.* Privacy has to do with pay-

ing attention to what is going on inside, of being aware of my total environment from the fall of light upon a field of wild flowers
to a stomachache. Privacy is being by myself, letting things
happen to me, or me directing my universe.

Taking one's self seriously is the first task of the autonomous
adult. This begins with the body, as the infant begins to notice
hand or foot. One of the most important tasks of privacy is to
make certain that body needs get met, so that the primary environment is secure, healthy, stimulated, and satisfied.

An overweight woman agreed that her biggest problem was
that most of her pleasure needs were met with food. It was only
when she took time to find pleasure elsewhere that she began to
relinquish her compulsion to eat. Among these were guitar lessons, a cat, and a return to sewing for herself, which inspired
her to lose weight. It is interesting to see how quickly people
with weight problems lose the pounds immediately after a divorce, when they are seriously considering how others, especially the opposite sex, see them.

In an outburst of anger, a young woman, who found herself
busy with her career as a veterinarian and the only custodian of
her crippled mother, became aware of neglecting herself. She
was able to focus attention on her own daily needs with the help
of a deck of 3 x 5 cards. I asked her to write a simple treat for
herself on each card, shuffle the pack, place them on her dresser,
and turn one up each morning as gifts to herself. They were
very inventive. Here are a few items on her list:

Take a short walk in the park.
Buy some fresh flowers or a new plant.
Listen to a favorite piece of music while doing nothing else.
Take at least a half-hour for a bubble bath.
Start a new book that I have been waiting for time to read.
Get up early and greet the sun.
Do something neat for my body.
Start judo lessons.
Buy a new perfume.
Move in "slow motion" today.
Go to lunch alone at a different restaurant and think about
    some of the lovely moments of my childhood.

> Write a poem for the first time since that creative writing
> course in college.
> Give some special attention to personal grooming.
> Start a savings account at the church credit union.
> Work on my picture album.

Occasionally her schedule prohibited carrying out the instruction on the card; so she simply put it on the bottom of the stack or somewhere along the way and tried the next one. Once she said she had two cards turned up "to keep a special couple of things in sight" rather than losing them back to the deck. She did not feel guilty when she could not treat herself. After three weeks or so she caught the habit, gave up the card dictatorship, and simply permitted a place in her schedule for a spontaneity that celebrated her. The exercise engendered an awareness of herself as a person worthy of special privileges and the ritual of privacy. She learned to take pleasure in herself and for herself.

It is not fair to expect someone else to love us if we cannot "make love" to ourselves. It is important not to do only an imaginary trip or simply to run errands for our daily support, such as buying vitamins or picking up the dry cleaning. We can give ourselves a treat that can mean as much as a present from a friend.

A single woman decided she had to learn to masturbate as a love gift to herself; she did this not out of desperation and loneliness, but in a new spirit of self-acceptance and a healthy appreciation of sensuality. At age thirty-two she was happily tearful as she recounted experiencing her first orgasm. She said, "It was as though I became a woman last night. Is that silly? If so, I confess it with a lot of good feelings of achievement and contentment. I thought I felt like a woman the night I lost my virginity, but this beat that by a mile."

Privacy comes out of a self-conscious desire to find oneself and experience oneself for information and delight. It is most often not public and has deeply to do with seclusion, secrecy, and solitude.

To discover self is the great frontier and probably the most exciting adventure available to each of us. Yet many people are made anxious in solitude. Body awareness can be frightening.

"I can hear my heart beating in my ears," someone will say. "I just get scared when I am alone." Suppressed anxieties may bubble to the top; respiration and heartbeat speed up, alarming the person even more, perhaps bringing on feelings of dizziness and panic. For some, being alone may trigger a mild hysteria.

It is clear that we want privacy; we are clear that privacy is a human need. It has been observed that we Americans will not give up our automobiles until *all* gas runs out. It is also doubtful that carpools will ever become popular. We like that brief private time in the car alone commuting or running an errand. Enclosed in those little spaceships of our cars we feel that the world, with its invitations, demands, and commercials – cannot reach us. We are immune for a time, often bathed in stereo music of our choice on tape. In therapy sessions people report turning up the "radio noise" and screaming back at it or swearing at the announcers. "It's all irrational," one man said. "It does not even respond to what's coming over the air. I just scream out my noise against their noise. I yell about things that happened that day, or just because I feel that way." Privacy functions differently for each of us. Auto privacy for this man was his occasion for ventilating his feelings.

Over the years I have talked with many mothers who manage time for themselves late at night when the house is quiet, children and husband asleep, and the demands of the day met or safely at rest. They take time then for a glass of wine and the newspaper already old. One woman said, "It is then as though the little bits of me that I have left all over the house and neighborhood come home. I knit back together. It's like getting to a favorite theme in a Beethoven symphony. So busy, then so exquisitely serene."

A part of the business of partnership is to help one another get the need for privacy met. Within that sphere are certain special gifts for the mind, body, and spirit that can only be given to oneself if adequate time and space are set aside. It is a partner's support of our need for privacy that often makes it possible. If the partner makes us feel guilty for wanting privacy or insultingly goes as far as one husband who asked, "What do you do in there all by yourself? That's the craziest thing I ever heard of," we can expect either fury or hurt from the mate, with a resulting chasm widening between the partners.

Some of us need privacy in order to write, read, practice an instrument, work in the shop, tinker with the car, paint, or take a walk. People can get awfully crabby over intrusions at those times. They may say, "You are interrupting my work, study, practice," but what they really mean is that you are interrupting their privacy, an unconscious need to be alone.

We must support one another's life goals found only in the realm of privacy. The health of the person and the relationship may depend upon how well privacy is attained in the marriage. "Leave me alone" may sound like an outraged misanthrope, when it is actually the legitimate cry of a spirit besieged. We must learn to listen for requests for privacy from our partner and then support that retreat. It is both a gracious and a loving thing to give. To have your partner volunteer, "I'll take care of that. Why don't you take a little time for yourself?" is a beautiful gift to receive, and too often it is a surprise.

Practice privacy. Learn to be alone. Cultivate a gentle solitariness. Sponsor and encourage it in your partner. Privacy is a time for remembering and savoring, for meditation upon the substance and truths of our lives, a time to fantasize and contemplate the future. It is a time to let down, relax, to be nothing and just be – to worship, to float, to dream. It is a time to enjoy – a time for one-on-one, you-on-you.

Intimacy

Eric Berne structured human use of time like a target, moving from withdrawal as space beyond the target to rituals, games, pastimes, work, and, finally, *intimacy* at the bullseye.

Yet, according to Claude Steiner in his book, *Scripts People Live*, Berne could not define intimacy, except as the absence of something else. Berne doubted that it is possible for anyone to attain intimacy, and, if it were, a person would be lucky to know fifteen minutes of intimacy in a whole lifetime. Why posit something so central to human relationships if it cannot be defined or experienced?

Intimacy, as I speak of it here, is reserved to describe a quality of relationship with another human being. I cannot be intimate with a pet rock. People have relationships of love and affection with birds and animals which they describe as intimate. I know these relationships exist, and I have no need for a semantic quarrel about the use of intimacy in this regard. Words are our servants. They change a bit sometimes in order to stay helpful. But I speak here of intimacy between people.

Intimacy is often the word used euphemistically for human sexual intercourse. Yet surely a couple could have intercourse and not be intimate. Further, if the substitution of *intimacy* for *intercourse* indicates something more than a mock modesty, we have assigned to mere coitus one of the noblest expressions defining depth in human meeting. Intimacy and coitus are not necessarily synonymous.

Still, I occasionally hear a woman report being forced by her parents to marry when the parents learned she had had intercourse. Years ago a woman told me that her father required that she marry her boyfriend when he caught them "having sex."

"I wasn't even pregnant. Besides, I didn't want to marry Bob. He did, but I didn't. You wouldn't believe the guilt feelings my father put on us. When I look back now, it's really funny. Not funny-funny, but laughable."

It was as though her father believed that intercourse caused some irrevocable union between a man and woman. When he caught them having intercourse, in his mind it was as though they had been fused in a mystical bond that was the most profound and holy experience given to human beings. Nothing could then separate them. She quoted her father as having said:

"Once that happens, there is no turning back. You belong to him and he belongs to you. That's as close as two people can get. Now you'd better start your wedding plans."

It is true that many people have the most intimate feelings during intercourse. They may feel *fully known*, as the word is used in Hebrew thinking on this subject, and they *know*. They feel loving and loved. Yet the two should not be confused. Intimacy has to do with the character of a relationship. Intercourse is coitus, a union of male and female genitals.

In the spirit of Alexander Lowen's theories of bioenergetics, especially as found in his book *Pleasure*, I believe that intimacy is a need that is very much a part of the body and its receiving systems. Most of us need to have our bodies accepted, appreciated, enjoyed, and loved. One might say:

> "I am in here, and it is impossible to separate me from my body. When you touch my body joyously, you touch me in ways that seem to say, 'It is good to be so close to you.' "

Sometimes it is almost a necessity to be embraced. There is a hunger for a hug, the most affirming gesture of the human family. To be whispered over, touched, and kissed – the barriers against the world's encroachment fall – we are tenderly laid bare in our quest for love; and like a deep breath, it cannot be saved for later. Intimacy is an ongoing, daily need.

That is why our world is so full of lonely people. They are emotionally starved. What is intimacy? Once at a workshop I asked the group for definitions and someone said, "Intimacy is privacy shared." This is like an oyster shell: a good place to make a pearl. It is a beginning and enables us to use what we have already said about privacy. It reminds us that real intimacy depends upon the quality of our privacy.

If I have loved *me* well, if I can feed my own spirit and take into my own hands my own body and not be ashamed, then I may be able to reach out without a crippling fear of rejection, share my private world, and receive another's. It is then that we begin to close the distance that makes loneliness and close the doors for a while against the loneliness of being creatures who can reflect upon our condition: to be human is to be alone. Intimacy is like fire upon the wood: a better way to be consumed in light and heat.

Intimacy is privacy shared. Relationships occur when we trust enough to participate deeply in one another's life. There is a sharing at the roots and of rooted things: ideas, dreams, feelings, and activities, so that a kind of transplanting comes about and we begin to appear in each other's lives. There may be only slight traces or dramatic metamorphoses, as we see the impact of one person's world upon another's.

The intimacy grows as *invitations* are given:

> This is a copy of a book I very much have enjoyed and I want to share it with you.

A few of my very best friends will be there and I am dying for
them to meet you.

I have never even thought of that sort of thing before. Give
me a little time.

expectations rise:

I told Robin that's the way you would feel about it. I'm so
glad you two talked.

I just would not have gone to the concert without you. Whom
would I have talked with about it?

It's a cinch my folks will be crazy about you.

closeness develops:

I like me better when I am with you.

You don't have to say a word. I know what's going on.

Please hold me. This has been one of those days. I just need
to be near you.

and *changes* occur:

It's a totally different experience with you.

The more we talk, the better I understand why you feel as
you do.

I'm sorry. I was really wrong. Thanks for being patient with
me.

Intimacy may occur within a variety of relationships.
Friends and relatives may be present in a special way and share
the deep concerns of our privacy so as to be intimately involved
in our lives.

A father said he felt like praying only with his young daughter as she said her bedtime prayers. This usually followed a brief
conversation in which they shared "the neatest thing that happened today" and "the worst." This was a time of intimacy.

Discovered by his wife in an affair, a military officer recalled
that the best thing about the experience with his lover was that
he could "talk and cry with *that* woman" when his daughter was
on drugs and he could not with his wife. "You don't know what
that meant to me," he said. His wife had insisted that they not
discuss it. "As far as I am concerned, she is dead," she had said.
The deeper intimacy was in the talking and crying together.

A woman who sat for months at the bedside of her daughter,
who was terminally ill with leukemia, said that when her husband sat across the bed from her, "I never felt so close to any human being in my whole life. He is a tender man."

Some people must find ways to break through great emotional barriers before they are free to engage in intimacy. I once asked a young woman, whose husband had demanded a divorce two years after marriage, how she got loved. She did not know what to say; so I invited her to close her eyes and fantasize a scene in which she might experience a moment of true intimacy with another human being. She sighed and relaxed. Immediately she looked troubled and tears came. When I asked her what was happening, she said, "I am about four years old. My daddy is home from Viet Nam. I am beside his casket with my mother and grandfather. My grandfather is holding me up so I can see my daddy. (*Long pause*) For some reason I feel very happy. I feel good. He is dead, but I feel good. I am not crying. That is, not in the fantasy." When I asked her to open her eyes, she said, "I'm glad you asked me to do the fantasy. I was not allowed to cry at the funeral. I feel closer to my father now than ever before." That fantasy marked the beginning of her movement away from bitterness and seclusion and into genuine experiences of intimacy.

It is expected that most needs for both grave and glorious human exchanges will be met within the partnership. Hopefully, the kindly passions of the spirit, from a hallowed grief to the most erotic sexual experience, will occur in the partnership as each gives trustingly and receives the other with genuine welcome.

Community

My community constitutes the network of people with whom I share my world. This is a broad definition. More personally, my community is essentially family and friends, who are the social fabric into which my life is woven. It is among them that I feel free to talk, play, create, work, and relax in an atmosphere of acceptance.

The *family* is a commune, a community. One's supportive communion should begin there. Robert Frost said that home is the place where, when you go there, they have to take you in. But the family experience should be more than "have to" responses. A young woman said, "I was thirteen before I realized that no one in our family even said good morning. It seemed incredible that five people—all of them older than I—could have lived together so long without even a 'hello' in the morning. So, I just started doing it. My father responded right off, but my mother and two sisters were still grumps, and would reply with something like: 'What's your problem?' or 'Don't be late for school now!' or 'What's so good about it?' It was as though they were embarrassed or something."

The family is our first community. The basic ingredients of community are given or denied in that setting: security, acceptance, personal regard, trust, support, forgiveness, loyalty, and love. Words. But in these words are the nuclear elements of community. Without these elements the child flounders, and only by some miracle will an autonomous adult emerge.

The partner attempts to reestablish and maintain a new base of community in the family or marriage. There, each person is aware of the *centripetal* forces that pick up the members of the expanding community and put them in orbit around the core experiences of the primary relationships, beginning with the parents and extending through the family to the revivifying partnership.

The families of origin are drawn into the marriage. They meet cautiously, angrily, or cordially in a convergence of forces with a potential for community or chaos: note the differing examples of the Capulets and the Montagues of Shakespeare's *Romeo and Juliet* and the Webbs and the Gibbs of Thornton Wilder's *Our Town*. Partners move back and forth between the two camps, making a path and leading the way for those who are often strangers, or collapsing under the pressure of prejudice and resentment. Generally, it is important that both partners be acceptable to both families. When they are not, there is apt to be alienation and considerable pain, if not tragedy.

It is helpful if partners facilitate acceptance for each other. Occasionally, one partner may be called upon to stand up for the other, making it clear where his or her loyalty lies, and what attitudes will or will not be tolerated.

A woman, who felt her three teenage children were not being very helpful in making her new husband feel welcome in their family, said, "Look, I'm sorry your father died. I loved him, too, more than you will ever know. But now Al is here and he loves you very much. I don't like loyalty tests, but if a line is forming in this house, I love all of you and I love him, and he is at the head of the line."

A man said, "It was disgusting to see my parents literally fawn over Melany after she converted, while her own parents loved both of us, even after she switched. You would have thought the world had come to an end when we married, and a year later my folks celebrated as though Melany had been raised from the dead. But, then we had our revenge. Melany had actually wanted to make the change. It was genuine, and my folks thought it was just for them."

Parents condition a marriage with signals of acceptance or rejection that can have enormous reverberations throughout the community. They can set up the couple for success or failure according to their attitudes, feelings, words, and behavior.

Partners are sensitive to each other's centrifugal, or expanding, network of relationships. This may include business associates, club members, clients, neighbors, and friends. It has to do with groups and institutions, as well as individuals who have deep personal meaning for the partner. It relates to bowling teams and church committees, painting classes and bridge clubs, tennis buddies and the book guild. In the multifarious expressions of the personality, each of us needs to identify what she or he is about in the community of persons who feed us and allow us to give to them out of our creative and celebrative depths. The community is our universe of public availability; we are like the artist who sets up an easel on the corner of a busy street where all can see the expression of the self in public, while at the same time going about one's task in a spirit of enormous, private satisfaction.

Partners participate in, encourage, create, and support community with and for one another. Couples in counseling report a variety of problems in this area:

The family is clearly not the top priority for the husband/ father. The wife and children become resentful, creating either a wobbly unit with the shadow father haunting their spirit and activities, or a group of floating human islands, touching and talking in wistfulness and anger.

A partner is jealous of the other's friends and activities

not shared in the marriage: friends at the office, a handball partner, bridge club, church functions, show dog owners, etc. Occasionally this has nothing to do with reasonableness, in that the other partner could "come along too," or that significant time is also invested in the partnership. It is simply a blind jealousy.

In a partnership of trust, such problems are more easily resolved if the quality of intimacy enables both partners to feel wanted and loved. Otherwise, it is hard to accuse someone of jealousy when that person feels neglected. Also, it is difficult to check out, since who is to say what is "enough" intimacy?

Jean addressed this subject with her busy husband and concluded, "All I'm asking is for just more of you. Not money. Not furs and jewels," she said with a plaintive smile. "Just more of you."

Dan's response was: "Okay. What do you want me to give up? Bowling? You want me to give up Tuesday night bowling? What am I going to tell the guys? 'Jean won't let me out on Tuesday night anymore; she says she wants more of me'? I can hear them laughing now—especially Hank and Tom." He was not smiling.

Such begging and protestations are usually symptoms of problems in the larger relationship—a game of "hide-and-seek," as we called it in chapter 2, in which one partner is always trying to find the other. In a stronger relationship, needs are announced, respected, negotiated, and satisfied, with breathing space left for each partner in his or her separate community activities.

In the expanding network of relationships, we both *discover* and *invent* ourselves. We are triggered, challenged, invited, and pushed into an infinite variety of experiences with all sorts and types of people. Each person in our community potentially offers us a different world. Entering that world, we not only encounter our friend, but we also are introduced to his or her world, peopled with others who share, in turn, bits of their world. They become fragmentary mirrors in which we get glimpses of ourselves moving through the space and time of our lives. It is in these exchanges that inventing and discovering occur and we grow. Communities are enriching and, in turn, the marriage is enriched. It may seem risky, but let each other go, and the returns are apt to be beautiful.

Transcendence

To transcend is *to go above, to overpass or exceed, to get beyond oneself*. In a general way, we are speaking here of an understanding of life that transcends the time and space limitations of privacy, intimacy, and community. We are concerned with questions dealing with the *meaning* of our existence. How do we attempt to "make sense" of life? What's it all about? Can we discover the purpose and ultimate goals for individuals and the whole human family? Does living finally matter beyond just staying alive and trying to enjoy it?

Religion, philosophy, and psychology have been quite self-consciously preoccupied with this search for meaning. In the *Logotherapy* of psychiatrist Victor Frankl, this search is central to both his system and the therapeutic process. His book, *Man's Search for Meaning*, was written out of his soul-crushing experience in Nazi prison camps. Miraculously, he survived when many others did not. His survival might be at least partly attributed to his belief that life is intrinsically meaningful; that is, simply to live is meaningful, but our living is enhanced by our search and discovery of the more personal and explicit meaning of our individual lives. Frankl believes that every person is engaged in this search. He suggests that we may discover the meaning of life in at least one of three ways: (1) through some important accomplishment; (2) through experiencing some value in nature or the culture, such as work or love; and (3) through suffering.

Abraham H. Maslow, especially in his books *Toward a Psychology of Being* and *Religions, Values and Peak Experiences*, has focused much of his thinking and research on what he calls the "peak experience," a transcending moment when a person is deeply moved in what may be an ecstatic experience that often leaves the person significantly changed in both attitude and action. These may be revelatory events in which we are shown something of the deeper meaning of our lives. We may, in them, be given direction or instruction concerning how better to explore and experience that meaning. It is assumed that the mystical experiences in the lives of the saints and spiritual leaders of history were absolutely critical to their revelations and reached to the core of their messages.

Frankl is centrally occupied with the search for meaning. Maslow focuses on what he calls his concept of *self-actualization*, which has to do with our becoming fully realized as persons. Again, Carl Jung called it *individuation*, realizing ourselves. For me to explore my experience as a thinking, feeling, acting, and believing human being is a search for meaning. The meaning of me is clarified and given unity when these come together harmoniously. These aspects of me – when integrated and made congruent – constitute the *me* that I am about. However, the poets and saints have insisted through the centuries that life is somehow more, and that more may be suggested in Maslow's *peak experience*. These bold moments of spiritual drama and revelation that confirm or open the way for us seem to come when we are struggling to bring unity of thinking, feeling, acting, and valuing to a point of belief and commitment. It is in this belief and commitment that we make promises, take risks, invest ourselves, and move out upon the way of growth, enrichment, and self-actualization.

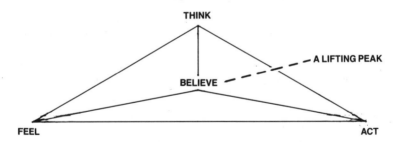

The peak experience becomes a transcending (mountain peak) event in which my integrating self rises above what is considered my "daily routine" and lifts me in a gripping movement of serenity and insight. Life becomes *four*-dimensional.

The story of Christ's temptation on the mountain at the outset of his ministry and the legend of Gautama Buddha receiving enlightenment under the Bo tree are two of the more familiar examples of this harmonizing, focusing, and committing process in the lives of great religious leaders. Similar events of meaning and enlightenment occur every day among men and women who take seriously their own pilgrimage, and who want to come to an understanding of themselves in the universe. Some seem to *actualize and individuate* in a yea-saying stance in which they say *Yes!* to life with affirmation and celebration. Others seem to be nay-sayers: life is realized in denial of things, or of intimacy, or even of reality. What we think life is, it is not. Just when we think we have discovered meaning, life is most meaningless. The search goes on. Some believe that the meaning of life is that life is nothing. H. L. Mencken is reported to have said that mankind is a fly on the wheel of the dung cart of the world. If that is true, we are of all creation the most miserable and deprived, and perhaps we deserve to perish.

The meaning question can sound abstract and removed from life. But if Frankl is correct in assuming that the search for meaning is what all of us are about, then the search is at the very center of life. The search goes on in the building of empires, in the monumental works of art, in great pioneering enterprises, as well as in the more modest activities of earning a living, growing hybrid roses, building a jogging record, changing jobs, studying star maps, abandoning old habits in search of a new experience, watching a tiny baby awaken, wondering about dandelions, avoiding the dentist, and just about everything else we do. All of life seems to fall broadly somewhere along the thrust-line of our lives, a line called *search for meaning.* This transcending quality of life stretches all the way from a dogwood blossom to Thornton Wilder's "Mind of God."

Even though the search goes on for each of us, we must find ways to declare meaning: my life means *this* at center, now. In a support group I once asked that we write our own obituaries in which we might suggest something of the meaning of our own life experience. Here are a few of our responses:

I have tried to become a first-rate educator.
I spent most of my life trying to discover the real meaning of
    intimacy with a woman.
I only wanted to enjoy it all in a healthy way.
I have worked hard at keeping life simple and honest, and it
    felt good doing that.

I suppose I just tried to "get it on" with God.

I have pursued music like an ardent lover. It searches my
    soul like a comet lighting the heavens.

Meaning? If there is any, I've missed it; but then it seems
    that I have missed out on just about everything anyway.
    Who knows what anything means?

It all comes down to a choice of gods: ZERO/ONE. God is
    either no-thing or everything. I haven't decided yet.

To say that the search for meaning is in everything we do is,
perhaps, to say that it is in nothing. Therefore, the process involved in the will-to-meaning has more to do with how we handle the material of our lives. For instance, a man said, "I have a
hard time appreciating 'good' music. Oh, I like it okay, I guess. I
prefer 'Country Western.' But this city needs an orchestra. I
support that. I give a good bit of money to it. Maybe if I do, it
will encourage others to do the same." It is a worthy thing to be
about. He is helping to create an environment for the appreciation of all music, including "Country-Western." Someone else
might not go about it this way. He does, and it adds meaning to
his world.

Partners are in the business of marriage in order to further
the welfare of both their separate and combined enterprises. To
be alert to each other's changing needs and goals is a primary
task of partnership, for it is in this intimate dialogue that support, encouragement, and fulfillment are most sure to come. It
should be clear that unless there is the covenant/contract commitment to the hard work of doing life together, the possibility
of either abandoning the other for a new friend or a better lover
is considerably increased. It is in this sense of the marriage as a
duly constituted, legal, working organism with realizable goals
shared with a partner that a man and woman are most apt to
feel the security and substance of their experience together. The
greatest partnership task of all is to assist one another in realizing a full and satisfying life.

All the pharmacology now available to assuage emotional illness, to relieve our depressions and obsessions and offer the
other "miracles of medication" still leave us with the eternal
question: What is the meaning of my life? The healing use of

prescription drugs is a little like sobering up a drunk so he can try to make a meaningful life. At most medication can only free us for the quest. Great partners walk and talk together in this search for meaning in their separate lives and in their life together.

Chapter 5

LOVERS SHOULD FEEL LOVED

A common expectation of marriage is that in it one has a guarantee of love. Friend and partner is under promise also to be lover. Of all the people in the world *this one* had pledged "to love and to cherish," no matter what words were used – traditional or contemporary. Words, symbols, and witnesses converge in a marrying way to give a seal of commitment, the assurance of a nurturing affection beyond any required elsewhere or expected from any other. "This one truly loves me!"

To some, these expectations are arbitrary and contrived, fatuous and like a sugar castle of improper demands, and absurd hopes. I once heard John Updike say that we "put too much on a marriage," expect more than any relationship can give. Nevertheless, we all try to slip past the rhetoric and poetry of the ceremonial love trysts and search the vast Niagara of messages from the lover for the clear assurance of unconditional acceptance and grace. More than all else, *this* one, *here, now* – love!

It is from this lover that the best of love is expected. It is in this celebration of the mating of us-persons that we hope to give love at a depth and with an extravagance that shall be for us a sign of arrival in a relationship of trustworthy and predictable devotion. Some believe that such mutually given promises will bring a new *wholeness* ("All I need is your love, and nothing can stop me"); *moral perfection* ("Love is the great commandment. Our love makes it possible for me to love all those other folks"); *bodily health* ("Our love invigorates me. The depression is gone"); *peace of mind* ("Life was hell until you told me you loved me, and suddenly I have enormous peace, a feeling that everything is going to be okay") In the years of my practice I have heard all of these and more from the very young in premarital counseling to middle-aged divorcees on a high adventure with new love. These paeans to the miraculous powers of love reflect our deep need to know that here is love in endless supply, an alchemists's dream of translating base to precious, like to love, I to we, now to forever. Yet, love at the gate of all-things-possible is more than a magic show. It is a birthing of something small and splendid, too fragile to go unattended, and too full of the promise of its parentage to be taken for granted. It is in this *promise* that hope resides: "I promise you, and hope to be able to keep those promises."

The love story begins to be written. If like most, it may be flawed and raveled, littered with broken promises and quickly mended dreams. Friendship keeps lovers talking and touching. Partnership helps them work at the contract, so that in the loving they may have hope, make it real. But as lovers they enter a mystery: the beckoning, analogue cloud-figures (It looks like) by day and the fire-spirit (We are one) by night that draws lovers on, not to some promised land in which all promises are realized, but to the next gift of love between them when life is made good, again and again. Those who love this way know its truth and ultimacy. They are the ones who are able to spoof their own love. And they are also the ones who are most apt to have enough to spare, and the ones most apt to share it.

In promise and hope is the making of love, not *out of nothing (ex nihilo)*, as in Hebrew thought, so much as *out of the available*, as in Greek thought. Our word "poet" comes from a Greek word which means to make or to fashion. How then do we make love happen for us?

"And how, my dear, do you know he loves you?"

This
He says so.
He acts like it.
He wants to marry me.
He is all I ever wanted.
He made love to me.

Or

My heart knows.
We act like lovers.
I feel loved.
I believe him.

Who knows? Either can be deceived. We look for a lodestone, a talisman, a formula – something that takes the guessing out of "How can we be sure?" *Making* love is no conjured thing, but something done in the time and space elements given to a man and woman for talking and touching. *Making* love is the keeping of old promises and making new ones. *Making* love is the fashioning of oneself in the presence of another so that both are loved, and feel that way.

Care

We begin with caring. Love is made in caring. To care for someone is to *pay attention* to that person. I am mind-full. I am care-ful not to be forget-ful, or else she may say, "Sometimes I feel you just do not care about me." I notice her, may call attention to her in ways that make her feel cared about.

A wife complained to her husband that she felt uncared about when he talked with his parents by long distance phone. "I have timed you and your folks talking for as long as thirty-five minutes without you so much as mentioning me once." It did his cause no good when he thoughtlessly said that his parents had not asked about her.

One of the great speeches in Arthur Miller's play *The Death of a Salesman*, occurs when Willie Loman's wife defends him to their ridiculing sons. Willie is out in the backyard "acting crazy" when his wife Linda reminds the boys that, even though Willie

has failed in so many ways, he is still a human being and their
father and he deserves better at their hands. She says, "Attention, attention must be paid." Regardless of our condition of
failure, all of us in relationships of intimacy expect basic regard.
We expect to be acknowledged, taken seriously, and as a woman
said, "more than noted in passing."

Caring *about* has to do with a sensitivity that enables us to
stay tuned to where the lover is noting, marking, and valuing
life, especially as it relates to one's person, property, and heart
interests. How do you measure caring?

So what's so special about a new hairdo?

It's only a car, dear, and can be straightened out.

I could cut off my beard and you would never notice.

If you really cared, you would call me when you know you will
be late.

I do care. It's just that I have a poor memory.

It's hard to care about you when you don't care about yourself.

If I *didn't* care, I wouldn't complain, dear.

Some people care too much, and they get hurt.

Caring about has to do with *awareness*. If I know what is important to you, within reason I will try also to make it important to me and will pay attention so that we do not have an "out
of sight, out of mind" relationship.

There is also a caring *for*. Lovers have ways of protecting, de-
fending, and nurturing one another. Illustrations come quickly
to mind: the television cliché of buckling up and locking car
doors; supporting the other in his or her no-smoking or dieting
program; encouraging the lover to return to school, or work, or
the home when that is a nurturing thing to do; and on and on in
those simple things that say I want you in my world feeling
happy and loved.

Perhaps it is important here to ask how we care *for* our lover
when she or he is ill. Over the years I have been surprised how
often this subject appears in a couple's laundry list of "You
never/You always." Some overdo and others underdo. Some lovers are resentful and petulant, scolding, "You should have listened to me and this would not have happened." Others hover
and nurse until they are a smothering nuisance. Caring *for* in
time of illness must be sensitively done, having to do not only

with the lovers' health conditions but also with their attitudes toward illness.

The way we handle illness for ourselves and others often affects relationships globally, that is, throughout the relational sphere. There are indications that some of us welcome illness to punish others in our life system or in order to meet the other's need to nurse and feel superior. Illness is seemingly motivated by more than microorganisms. Illness may then become a manipulation whereby we have various other needs met, some of which may appear to be absolutely necessary for a particular style of relationship to be ongoing. Research appears even to suggest that certain kinds of heart attacks and other crippling illnesses that render a person dependent may often be locked in to unconscious perceptions of needs within the intimacy circle for one to take care of or be taken care of.

There is a subtle movement from caring *for* to taking care *of*. The latter—at least for me—suggests something close to a mother/child or nurse/patient relationship, and it implies considerable dependency. Times of such need occur in marriage. Yet I think it helpful to maintain a distinction between caring for and taking care of, even if that distinction sounds contrived and artificial. I make this suggestion because there is the danger of a critical loss of dignity when one is taken care *of*. If I care *for* someone, I attempt to maintain a dialogue between my highest center of human dignity and that of the other. If I take care *of*, I may tend to take charge in such a way as to cause the other to say, "What's the use? He will not pay attention to me anyway."

The reports coming out of such dependency suggest feelings of being trapped, a victim of the illness and the nurse's disposition (male or female), even to the conclusion, "I might get well if it were not for you." Indeed, it appears that people have been kept ill by those who need to take care of someone. My point is supported by numerous stories of survival of the seriously ill because someone quit blindly taking care *of* and started caring *for* a patient. There are the heartbreaking stories of persons who tell of their fear in the face of an indifferent, mindless administration of medicine and procedures, as compared to the quiet presence of a truly aware and caring person at the bedside, saying in a thousand ways, "I care *for* you."

In marriage, "take care of me" is a child-to-parent request or command that implies a *piggyback* or *clutch* style. As shown in chapter 2, these styles are unhealthy even if some marriages can survive only in such modes. There are other options, perhaps the best going something like this: "I will take care *of* me, so that you may care *for* me in my need as we both see it."

There is another caring area – caring *with*. This has to do with the careful sharing of relationships and values within the marriage. For example, a wife complains that her husband takes little time with their nine-year-old son. The husband makes excuses. He announces them as though they are sound, valid reasons. The job is especially heavy just now. The son always seems to be busy or has other plans every time the husband suggests something to do together (as he has perhaps twice in the last six months, and then at the last minute). The wife recalls that once after supper the husband had asked their son, "How would you like to go to the ball game tonight?" The son had swimming plans with his friends. Assuming his hurt look, the husband then turned to his wife with raised eyebrows as though to say, "Well, you can't say I didn't try." After the son left the table, the argument began between husband and wife:

She: Don't you care about Timmy?
He: That's a ridiculous question. You know I do.
She: Then show him that you care. I feel he is totally my responsibility. Sometimes I feel like a single parent. I get lonely and frightened at having to make almost all of the parent-child decisions. And I get angry with you when I have to do all of the discipline. It's unfair. I am the ogre and you are Santa Claus who brings presents back from trips, then takes off to play golf with his friends.

This wife is saying care *with* me. Show that you are in this *with* me, share the fun and responsibility of parenthood and be supportive of the extra load that as mother I willingly carry. The partner is needed here in the contracting and doing of the parenting team, but the lover who cares *with* is needed even more. The woman needs a man who is closer to a lover, doing the loving thing with the offspring of their love. A neighbor could take the son to the ball game. It is a different feeling for both mother and son when the father takes him in a caring *with* spirit for the wife and caring *about* for the son.

These prepositional distinctions may seem unnecessary. They are not. People get lost from each other. These little parts of speech point back to relational values. The wife needs real support, and the boy needs loving attention.

In summary, I want to share an acrostic that has proven helpful to people trying to clarify the care concept in marriage. As we move down this list of four words, we move deeper into the core of the caring. At the top we carry each other's burdens. At the bottom we inspire one another with enthusiasm for life and life together. In a great love, it feels as though we breathe life into each other with our deepest gifts of caring.

C   Suggests *carry*. I am prepared to take on your burdens when they are more than you can bear. I will get under it with you or for you. And since I care about you, I will surely carry my own weight at all times, unless I am smitten.

A   Suggests *accompany*. We are together, in concert, each one carrying his or her own part, like the voice and piano in harmony. I move with you and you with me. We pair, match, blend, and mate. We do our own thing *together*.

R   Suggests *resonate*. I pick up the "vibes" of your life, and try to respond on the right note. You turn on my world and I vibrate to you. We are on the same wavelength.

E   Suggests *enthuse*. From the Greek, *en Theos*, it means to infuse a divine spirit. We awaken each other's lifeforce, and our spirits so indwell one another that we feel the movement and power of what each is about, and we share that with excitement and happiness. We breathe life into one another.

Cherish

This word is too seldom found in books about marriage. Women often seem to understand the word better than men. Yet, even among women it is too rarely used. Perhaps cherish is a word too vague, subjective, poetic – perhaps even a little too precious. In the gutsy language of pornography, the sterile no-

menclature of sex manuals, and the hip talk of sock-it-to-me
sex, most of the cherishables get lost; they become perishables.
It may then take an enormous personal effort if we are to transcend the science and slobber of our sexual stupor. If we do not
soften to death in the slow glue of Hollywood's latest love story,
we can experience again something of the lyric quality of genuine love.

Despite its virtual absence in studies of marriage as a quality
of relating, cherish appears often in the literature of love – poetry, ballads, love songs – as part of the bittersweet fantasies of
lovers *in* love. Its Latin root *carus* (dear) is also the root for the
French *cher*, and for our word *caress*. Dictionaries usually converge on "to hold dear" as a start toward defining *cherish*.

When we move from care to cherish in love, we have moved
from the gardener's looking *after* to the poet's looking *into* with
fantasy and feeling. Fantasy embellishes the beloved, and the
feelings are an inspired passion that begins early to call for celebration in the genital embrace. Looking into has inspired poets
across the ages, even before the Song of Solomon down to this
present time to sing about the lover as beautiful, virtuous, de-
voted, and unique. Such a person may be best described as *treasured*.

Cherish is not an empty word. Whenever I have mentioned it
before an audience, the women smile knowingly. It conveys
something that other words miss. It creates an ambience all its
own. I have asked some of these people what the word connotes
to them, and how they recognize the feeling of being cherished.

> It's in the eyes – the way he looks at me. I go all soft inside.
> Not like jello-soft, mind you. More like honey. Yeah, cher-
> ish is all *eyes*.
> Cherish is surprise. Serendipity. Beautiful surprise. Some-
> thing over and beyond the call of duty. Like the way my
> husband made me feel when I told him I was pregnant
> with our fourth child and was not at all sure I wanted to
> be. He understood my feelings, even though he disagreed.
> He held me and I felt cherished.
> The only time I ever *felt* cherished was in a dream just before
> I married (I'm divorced now). We were walking in a spring
> meadow, holding hands and laughing. I felt so good – inno-

cent and free – like there was nothing to do but what we were doing, and that was the best of anything to do. It all seemed so unreal, like a scene from *Elvira Madigan*.

Cherish is a thief. It steals away reality and leaves a sweet aftertaste that turns brown. So if you ever feel cherished, gargle.

Cherish is to have and to hold. Like a swat on the bottom that says, "That's mine." (The group cries "MCP"!) She replies, "MCP, hell! I swat him more than he does me."

Cherish is a woman's word. We both got goose-pimply when you were talking about it. But she's turned on and I'm cold, scared. Sounds heavy, like poetry the way you said, and I gave that up in high school.

I agree with whoever said cherish is all eyes, so long as she will let the hands slip in there a little bit. I think you should say more about cherish as caress.

I think to be cherished is the most perfect love there is – the way pomegranate is *the* fruit for me, the way sky means blue, and all roses are really red down under. Love is cherish. How does it feel? Like the ice cream I had after my tonsillectomy when I was eight.

It is poetry. I felt most cherished when my husband used to send me poems – his poems, before we were married. They were full of his feelings for me – some of them were things he has never said since. I felt really special, like Number One, somebody like nobody else could be to him. I wish he would write me poems again.

A number of things usually emerge when people begin talking about cherishing. (1) People have trouble sharing their feelings about feeling cherished by someone. It is very personal and private. (2) Everyone's experience with those feelings is different. Some have felt cherished but it did not last, and there was what one person called aftertaste. I am always aware of the humor associated with being cherished and am not sure whether the feelings happen that way or embarrassment causes the relieving humor. (3) The cherished feeling generally seems to associate itself with qualities of sweet, tender, often erotic, acceptance. (4) That acceptance is not only unconditional, it is without comparison: "I'm Number One." Most of us yearn for this, to be preeminent in someone's life, the most important other. Second-among-equals for lovers is not possible for most of us. We want to be first, among no other equals. (5) For others, cherish suggests feelings of being adored, revered, prized, and esteemed, all words that express an elevation of feelings to the point at which one seems to be of extraordinary worth. If it is not parasitic or idolatrous, having such feelings as a gift of another's love can be a beautiful and enhancing thing. To be healthy and effective, however, it must be mutually given, each to the other.

My wife recalls as a little girl asking her Aunt Marjorie why she polished her silver. "Does it make food taste better?" Marjorie laughed and said, "No, I guess I just like to see it shine." There is something about cherishing that is like that; it is not so much practical as caring, more to see the glow and feel the warmth of such awareness and recognition of the other.

If cherish is a woman's word, men should pay attention, because we need to know what the feeling is that they so enjoy and because we need it too. Perhaps men shy away from it because of its quality of tenderness. Perhaps cherish suggests to some men an absolute commitment that makes them feel trapped. Perhaps it is the intensity of the feeling which cherish elicits that troubles us. Perhaps it is none of these, and we are simply unfamiliar with the word as a working word of love. After all, how many words do we use for love in our man's world? Hardly any at all.

I believe in both the power and the magic of words. If communication is talking and touching, we need something like words to get our message across. Cherish is one of those words. It is a heart word. Like a magnet it can gather new, tender feelings in us, perhaps feelings just taking shape, creating enough energy for us to fantasize what we may offer our lover as a gift of *I cherish you.* Such a fantasy or daydream may begin just now as an exercise in learning to give the gifts of cherishing. It is to be hoped that such a beginning would lead to greater spontaneity, so that at the heart of the relationship is the frequent, generous giving of such a love. What causes your lover to feel most cherished?

Once in my office a wife was strongly criticized by her husband because it took her such a long time to reach orgasm when they made love. They had long since given up on the possibility of it occurring during intercourse. So, after he climaxed he methodically caressed her genitals. He became weary and sleepy after twenty minutes or so. The interesting point in the story came when I asked her how she felt during those minutes and she answered, "Fine." She was straight, not sassy. Despite her husband's complaints, she was enjoying it all. Gently, I then suggested that perhaps she was unconsciously delaying her orgasm in order to extend their time of closeness, since his practice was to climax quickly, roll over, and go to sleep because she always "had trouble coming." It was a revelation to her and she seemed relieved to understand what had been going on. She had solved her need for contact by creating yet another problem.

It is sad when we cannot tell our desires openly to one another and expect a helpful response. We often feel most cherished by the way we are held.

Celebrate

Life should be decorated throughout with celebratory events. Most of us manage to pay attention to the festivals: rites of faith such as baptism or bar mitzvah, national and religious holidays, and even to unique anniversaries such as the day we opened our own shop or came home from the war. We are likely to continue family traditions on certain special days, such as Halloween, Mother's Day, or the reunion trade-offs on Thanksgiving and Christmas, where we often eat and drink too much, play competition – the family game of most-is-best, using pieces called jobs, money, cars, boats, and children. But mostly, families seem to enjoy reunions and try to make them celebrations.

In my childhood home we celebrated seven birthdays: those of our parents, us four sons, and June 12, the birthday of our family, as my parents called it, the day of their wedding. My mother and father lived to be 79 and 94, respectively, and no matter how far we sons strayed from their home over the years, we never forgot that date, congratulating our parents with calls and cards, so that even today when June arrives, the twelfth always jumps out at me as a special day of thanksgiving and celebration.

Love finds its character in caring, its heart in cherishing, and its soul in celebrating. Soul is psyche, spirit – the living, breathing essence of personhood. Celebration is the great integrating power of every human being who cries, "All is well!" Celebration emerges out of and brings with it a feeling that *life is good*, which is our noblest human response.

Celebration may be attempted at times other than when life is good, when life in fact is not good or is being experienced that way. These are celebrations of memory (how it was) or of fantasy (how it might be).

Genuine celebration of the soul is ecstasy (to stand outside of), when we are apt to feel transported, lost, out of this world. Alexander Lowen, in his book *Pleasure*, cautions that real ecstasy is not painful, but exquisitely pleasurable. Creative celebration gives wings for soaring, from which we are brought back to earth better grounded, with new feelings of buoyancy and hope and a clearer resolve about the intent and direction of our lives. The spirit expands and dreams, makes space for breathing and motion, flexes body and mind, and perhaps for an interval slips out of time and feels at home with the universe. These can be quiet moments. They often come privately for me when I am sailing, writing a poem, or just lying in the backyard watching the woodpeckers and squirrels flitting in the high-vaulted treetops of oak, ash, and maple. Right now the breeze is playful. The sun is quite warm and flecking through the branches. There is a spirit of peaceful celebration: life is good!

Destructive celebration, historically called orgy, deadens the spirit, is at most distractive and escapist, tends to become an end in itself, and fails to equip us for living. It cannot be called celebration at all. It is a defamation of the human spirit and of any "life is good" concept. It more often seems to say, "Life is so bad, but this is the only way we are able to survive."

Some people live life with such a vengeance that they are left jaded and depressed, so that a quick blast of narcosis from alcohol or other drugs seems like the easiest and surest way out of the pit. But they never get out. Nothing changes except their awareness. Things look different, but they aren't, and later they pick up the new day with the same old fatigue and disenchantment. It is a winding down, grinding down way to do life. The only hope is some real attempt at creative celebration.

Love thrives on celebration. Love may survive without celebration. Like scrub pines in poor soil, it may persist in the face
of enormous calamity against ferocious winds at the edge of a
rocky tree line. But love flourishes best in creative celebration.

Lovers celebrate their love. We do this best by celebrating
ourselves as aware, autonomous persons and by celebrating the
other in caring and cherishing ways that make both of us feel
loved, stimulated, and enjoyed. Such times, in marriage, can
come in a moment and for the taking if we are awake and our
spirits not eroded. But such times might better also be *planned*
as something to look forward to, and to make sure that those
times of respite, abandon, and relaxed aliveness are a vital part
of our way of life and not just chance happenings. Some couples
find it helpful to spend at least one hour together each day or
evening, at least one major four-hour period every weekend, a
long weekend once a quarter, and half of the family's vacation
time if they have children. Separate vacations are sometimes
appropriate. These time frames seem necessary to the health of
a married relationship. A couple can build in more time as it is
available.

Yet, couples still find excuses: there isn't enough money; we
can't find babysitters; time is our problem; and – worst of all –
there just doesn't seem to be that much to say to each other. We
usually do what we *want* to do. If people take their children
everywhere they go, spend every weekend with his folks or hers,
only go out with other couples, and reduce all fun time together
to "What does it cost?" I assume that they really do not enjoy
each other very much, and in some real way they want to avoid
each other and avoid facing that fact.

My fear is that we have not yet understood the place and
need for celebration in marriage. We have had work models,
models for children, religious models, survival models, success
models, and others. Yet, in all of these there has been little room
for celebration. Small successes, such as a child bringing home
good grades, are still reported to me as being ignored by parents
or dismissed with, "That's what you are supposed to do." There
may not even be a word of congratulations, much less genuine
praise and some simple celebration. Our models may include going out, having friends or relatives over, or a party now and
then, but I am speaking for a spirit, an attitude that *demands*

that life and love be celebrated. The parties and going out may
very well be celebrations. The most important thing is that we
enjoy these events, that they leave us feeling "up" and refreshed,
and as a couple they help us to feel closer rather than alienated,
more loved than rejected.

Assuming that celebration is a good thing, that every couple
needs it, and that it really is fun, how do we do it? Again, it is
important to remember *privacy, intimacy, community,* and
transcendence as modes or spheres in which we experience the
exhilarating exclamation: life is good! Without this movement
through the four basic areas of human response, it is difficult if
not impossible to have a genuinely celebratory spirit in a marriage. A subtle and exciting interaction occurs between and
among all four.

There are two basic movements through them. One, I call the
crescendo movement when a life-is-good affirmation begins
with the self, moves into at least one truly intimate relationship, and moves outward to others with whom life is truly good,
climaxing in a declaration to the universe that in this moment
living is good. The second is what I call a *movement of grace.*
Celebration may occur in one area when it is impossible for us to
feel that life is good in another. This has been one of the hall-
marks of every good religion; it gives us *passage* – albeit not
free passage, as Bonhoeffer warns us about cheap grace – out of
the death sphere into the life sphere. It is opting for life rather
than death. This is resurrection.

The Hebrew-Christian literature is filled with examples of
such grace. This movement of grace may be the chief thing that
keeps us sane. When life in the private sphere seems over-
whelmingly tragic, or absurdly comic at best, and there is little
spirit for celebration, another who lives close to our world, who
knows and loves us, is often able to redeem that pain with love
and call us into celebration. The community of the believers in
every faith is for many a support fellowship whose love embraces with such tenderness and assurance that life there becomes good. Self-worth may be uncovered in that company;
perhaps a relationship of intimacy is created so that love makes
a home in us, and in the most transcending ways life becomes
fulfilling, meaningful, and celebrative. Perhaps it is not over
against or in spite of, but *because of* the work of religious communities that we have discovered in more recent years that the

so-called secular communities are also able to give meaning and celebration to life. Regardless, it would appear that celebration must occur throughout the life range for one to make a full and vital commitment to life as essentially and ultimately good. The acceptance of death as more than "the bitter end" depends upon some transcending celebration of the fundamental glory of all creation and one's small place in it. Despite the childlike spirit of such sentiment, I do share life with the butterfly who has but one day, with that fantastic whippoorwill outside my window this moment, and with the extravagant cascade of roses dying upon the fence, and I celebrate. Life is *good*. Nature is capricious and violent. Men, women, and children can be cruel, often are, and spoil life for themselves and others. But still, *life* is good. It is a worthy human task to help more people experience it that way. Even though history is strewn with corpses of those who died in our grisly battles over definitions of the good life or the good person, I believe that we are further along in our struggle with people and the environment toward the celebration of life as fundamentally good for the whole of creation.

The way we celebrate depends on such things as our origins, values, tastes, and lifestyle. The merger of two personal patterns of celebration in marriage can be exciting. It may also create problems, especially if values are threatened or feelings abused by embarrassment or disappointment during those celebratory events. For example, the community and transcendence spheres can cause conflict in marriage, especially as they relate to loyalty and commitment expected by national origin, familial, racial, or religious groups. The celebrations of "life is good" can be radically different, for example, in Christian and Jewish homes, or, for that matter, among the various branches of either. It is only in acknowledging the best of each that the couple can reap the rewards of entering into each other's celebrations.

The central concern of this section is celebrating love *in marriage*. We have seen that a basic understanding of celebration is that it is a joyous statement that life is good. In marriage it is, "Life *with you* is good." Definitional statements are difficult to make since each couple's model is unique and not apt to fit any stereotype. Still, there are at least three universals to be noted. Celebrative love in marriage is characterized for most

couples as *sensual, sexual,* and *genital,* as expressed most profoundly in intimacy arising out of a healthy privacy and finding
expression in both community and transcendence. Members of
the couple's community will see *muted* expressions of their sensual, sexual, and genital celebration and know that it is not a
neutered marriage. A couple's life-statement as to the meaning
of marriage (transcendence) may also reflect the sensual, sexual, and genital celebration in the sphere of intimacy. Couples
reflect the value they place on their uniqueness as man and
woman, their respect for that uniqueness, and their pleasure in
it. This is evidenced in their behavior, be it in an elevator or a
church. It says, "Notice how they talk and touch, how they support and enhance each other's sexual identity. They like being a
man and a woman and they like it together even more. It's a
good bet they know something about making love." Rather
than, "They never really talk and touch. They fight like a cobra
and a mongoose. If either were the last man or woman in the
world, you could cancel the next generation."

Sensual

The sensual celebration of love has to do with the five senses
and our ability to use them to experience and communicate
pleasurable feelings for ourselves and our lover. It is therefore
imperative that intimacy permit a maximizing of the sensual
experience – that is, our ability to stimulate the five senses in a
play event in which we see, touch, hear, smell, and taste that
which enhances the pleasure factors of closeness. Body pleasure
is essential to emotional health and ego fulfillment. We must
play and feel good if we are to work and be well.

Time, place, and *energy* are primary components for setting
the stage for most celebrations. Unless we make time, prepare
an environment, and have the energy for meeting, there is little
likelihood of much happening. Giving another our *time* is a precious gift. It is probably the thing most often requested by a
husband or wife in marriage counseling. To offer time in a place
in which we are most apt to meet at a depth is – after years of
the cliché "backseat sex" – an added bonus. But to give time in a
supportive environment when my energy is still flowing strong
focuses these three principal elements for the greatest possibil-

ity of pleasure. However, sensuous exchanges may occur in many different places, at odd times, and at various levels of energy.

Part of the nature of celebration is breakout – celebrating when and where least expected, which can be the crucial factor in certain celebrative events. A couple reported driving home exhausted from an extended meeting of intercity agencies in a great metropolitan center at the height of the racial struggles. Passing a beautiful reflection pool and fountain, they stopped and went splashing through the sparkling water at one o'clock in the morning like children chasing a pied piper, finally falling down and rolling around in the water until both were soaked through and exhausted from tickling and laughing. Tempted to make love under the dogwoods, they restrained themselves, because of the traffic, and went home in their sopping clothes to the privacy of their own backyard lawn.

Alex Comfort's book *The Joy of Sex* and its sequel are full of sensual delights that titillate and arouse. However, there are many body pleasures that need not lead to intercourse, that, perhaps, *should* not. A complaint often heard in marriage counseling is that simple body pleasures too frequently serve merely for genital arousal and are not enjoyed for themselves. When a wife frets that when she turned the garden hose on her husband in the yard one day and he practically raped her, and he does not deny it, the problem need not be getting even or latent hostility, but simply the husband's inability to play. He might have grabbed the hose and doused her. Instead, it served only as a potent signal or stimulant for intercourse against her will.

As a little film classic so well portrays, a couple eating an orange together – all the way from examining the fruit to licking juice from the fingers – can be a feast for eyes, nose, mouth, hands, and ears (Mmmm!). Only the limits of imagination can exhaust the list of possibilities available to the individual and the couple in giving the body a sensory treat. The body likes to *move* (even more than it likes weights, push-ups, etc.): dancing, walking, running, swimming. It likes *aromas* – from its own and the lover's body essence to exotic perfumes, as well as nature's own fragrances in flowers, fresh-cut grass, bread, cheese, sea spray, a wooded glen, a plowed field, October in an apple barn, farmyard odors, pine resin, and on forever. The body likes *sounds* – from a baby's tiny sleeping sounds to the roar of mountain streams. It likes *touching* all sorts of textures and can distinguish a grain of sand or an eyelash; and it likes *being touched* – warm and cool, soft and hard, tapping and stroking. The body likes to *taste*: the tongue is an army of little samplers. The variety and harmony of flavors are parts of any gourmet's delight. It likes to *see* – shape, form, substance, color, size, distance, the calm, the storm, muted darkness, sunrise, moon glow, other eyes, the human body, fantasy.

A body experience that is very in-body and terribly sensual is fantasy. Like a dream, a fantasy can enliven the body so that it believes what it is seeing and experiencing in the fantasy.

Fantasy

The next time you travel a boring turnpike with little traffic, in fantasy imagine yourself outside the car:

feel with your hands the gravel at the edge of the pavement, the difference in temperature from pavement to earth, the prickly touch of mowed grass stubble on the road shoulders, the bark of trees, and the sharp barb of wire fencing;

smell the creosote on the posts, the musky under-bridge odor, the fruit-tree blossoms, the dead animal alongside, the clover (and honey, miles away);

hear drones, buzzes, blops, whistles, songs, and whooshes of things seen as in a silent movie from your car;

stretch all the senses, bathing your body inside and out as you become totally immersed in the outside environment;

and after fifteen minutes you may emerge from this trip refreshed, amused with the distraction, and delighted.

Fantasy

Using individual sets of earphones, listen with your lover to a recording, something long enough to create its mood. When the record is well underway, take off the earphones and experiment with letting your awareness move back and forth from inside to outside and return: eyes open, eyes closed, touching, not touching, etc. Something else, something more happens to the senses when you take off the phones and are greeted by silence, or the sound of crickets, the city, or your own whispers. It is different than just turning off the stereo. The earphones transport you. It is as though the room has not participated in the sound. A deaf man could not have touched the walls and felt the vibrations. To come out of the music, into the room, and back again (with the sounds still in your head) creates shifting sensations in the mind combined with a very different meeting outside, like stepping out of the shower into the waiting arms of your lover.

Fantasy

Just upon going to bed, close your eyes and imagine yourself naked in a beautiful pool in which you are assured of privacy. Surround the pool with exotica—flowers, birds, statuary, music, trees, and fish in the water. Move in the water in ways that will maximize the body experience, emphasizing the water event. If you do not swim or if you fear water, all the more reason to enjoy the fantasy. Dive to the bottom of the pool and feel the water temperature and the currents change. See the beautiful fish and electric eels. Hear the music under water. Touch the cool rocks and white sand. Be there! Caress your body with your hands. Enjoy. Drift off to sleep.

These fantasies allow the imagination to create sensations that actually enliven and accept body awareness. We know the power of dreams to terrify, move to tears, or bring to sexual orgasm. Fantasy is also able to generate body feelings, have extraordinary strength to stir or quiet the body systems and deeply touch the psyche, the central control agency of the whole person. Fantasy is one of numerous ways to give ourselves sensuous, celebrative moments, and all that is required is a willing imagination.

Lovers play "Do you remember?" games recalling body feelings:

That was the coldest water we ever swam in.
I can still taste the champagne.
The only sounds I remember are his singing and your saying, "I do."
The flowers at Kensington smelled like heaven.

Lovers can also do fantasy together in concert, mixing their impressions and feelings as though they were jointly telling a story. That way you share imaginary gifts that are pleasurable and stimulating. The input may both surprise you and support your own reverie. It will undoubtedly reveal where your mind plays and how well your body responds to your pictures and those of your lover.

Sexual

It is easy to see how at least two of the above fantasies might become explicitly sexual. That's fine. I have divided celebration into sensual, sexual, and genital experiences in order to say a number of things, among them being that the first (sensual) or second (sexual) need not lead to the third (genital). Such a statement may seem unnecessary, but some people still avoid the pure experience of the five senses, or avoid being in the world as a sexual adult because something or someone has taught them to be afraid of good feelings, since those feelings frequently lead to "something worse," or a vague "you know what," or, boldly, intercourse.

The noblest human posture demands that we be in the world as sexual adults. To deny our sexuality is to cripple the whole person. "Male and female created He them" is one of the oldest poetic ascriptions to form, figure, and life on this planet. In these sexual crowns are reflected other dualities: sun-moon, Yin-Yang, light-dark, soft-hard, poetic-rational, and so forth. We share with all of the more sophisticated life-forms the absolute inter-dependability of male and female. In most instances *the growing apart and coming together* represent the thrust of the total life effort – the central, organizing principle of plant and creature.

Since it was not very long ago that we survived our "unisex period" in this country, when long hair and jeans were everywhere and the muting of sexual distinctions seemed to represent a conscious effort to confuse the sexual stereotypes, it is important to note two things: (1) sexual stereotypes are an attempt to maintain custodial and functional differences (men do this, women do that), while, at the same time, (2) true stereotypes seriously threaten the marvelous gifts of our uniqueness.

We are all male *and* female. There is a point in gestation when every embryo is unisexual. Then each appears clearly female and would emerge with female genitalia, except when appropriately a chromosome carrying the genetic code signals "boy" and the male hormone, testosterone, commands that the basic female embryo become male. Afterward, it is the preponderance of male or female hormones that continues to support the sexual differences and their functions. Hence, *anything* – symbol or function – that we call male or female is potentially or actually present in both man and woman.

Here is a little puzzle by which we can sift out the "heavyweight" in sexual stereotyping. The following are twenty characteristics that our culture usually assigns to male and female. Place a number by each word in both columns as you feel you possess that characteristic, giving the following weight to each word: Strong-4; Mild-3; Weak-2; Absent-0. Then total each column.

Male	Female
aggressive	affectionate
ambitious	compassionate
assertive	gentle
athletic	loving toward children
competitive	loyal
dominant	sensitive to others
forceful	sympathetic
independent	tender
self-reliant	understanding
willing to take a stand	warm
Total _____	Total _____

The best balanced scores are those that fall between 35 and 40 in each column; that is, when a person is close to strong in all the above characteristics. For a man to score weak to zero in most of the traits under the heading *female* is to make him a male stereotype heavyweight, and weak to absent in at least ten of the most critically human factors of character and personality. The reverse is true for females. If we accept the notion that there are custodial and functional differences between male and female and that these differences survive in the best interests of the human race, we must at the same time insist that wherever possible both sexes share in the expression of the fascinating versatility of human creatures in all the communication systems of our interaction. If I as a male do not participate in what is called a female quality, I am impoverished in my own experience and crippled in my expression. "No man is an island unto himself" – flowing through every cell of his being is the awesome female hormone, progesterone, imprinting man with woman.

One of Carl Jung's major intellectual efforts was to track down and understand what he called the *anima* (feminine) and the *animus* (masculine). He suggested that the outward face that we present be called the *persona* (the mask). The inward face for males is the female *anima*, while for females it is the male *animus*. Jung believed that to be psychologically healthy, men must express their feminine side and women their masculine. Two excellent books on this subject have been written by Robert A. Johnson. One is titled *She*, and the other is *He*. Using the great, classic myths and mythical figures, Johnson has movingly described the complex workings of what we think of as the mystery of human sexuality in man and woman.

Perhaps one of the most helpful studies in this area is June Singer's *Androgyny*, in which she explores the concept of androgyny as it "involves recognizing the eternal flux of these opposing energies" best understood by most of us as masculine and feminine. Comprehending and celebrating the presence of these dualities helps us to become whole creatures and also gives unity to our symbolic and mythic world.

We are left, then, with the considerable problem of *focus* and *balance* in distinguishing the sexes. *Focus* is perhaps best described as the ability of males convincingly to celebrate being men, and females convincingly to celebrate being women. Neither sex will feel neutered so long as the other is convinced, and each is fulfilled as man or woman in the presence of the other. For men and women to feel fulfilled at a given level of interactions is perhaps the simplest test of mature adult sexuality. This fulfillment has to do with being perceived, accepted, understood, and appreciated as a man or as a woman by the opposite sex. It may be a simple exchange with a clerk in a store when somehow the "essence" of one's sexuality is received/exchanged and we are known in the moment as man or woman.

Needless to say, such perceptions do not emerge from vacuums. For a man to say to himself in the above illustration, "Now, there's a woman!" means that he has automatically processed millions of signals from his environment as to what a woman is. Ignoring the obviously freakish exception, when a man or woman with distorted notions of the nature of man and woman meet and affirm each other, I believe that we must simply trust this process of a man feeling like man (fulfilled) in woman's presence (and vice versa) as the best criterion we have for adult sexuality. For it is in this exchange that the business that a man and a woman have with each other will get done – physically, spiritually, psychologically, intellectually, and socially. The relationship is constantly evolving, and man and woman are discovering what each needs of the other and what each can give in order to put together the most fulfilling relationship possible for both and integrally for the human family.

"Orders from on high" less and less affect what men and women must "get done" together. God, church, and tribe have rapidly lost voice in terms of dictating the nature of the male-female exchange. One new direction now is coming from the state, which – in its ongoing process of self-deification – conditions our prerogatives in the most personal and intimate spheres of life. For example, the day may come when a couple must obtain a license in order to have a child, just as India has already begun enforcing sterility after a person has mothered or fathered a third child. In China, only one offspring per couple is permitted. The focus of sexuality today has to do with the ability of men and women to realize their greatest possible fulfillment now at this point in the journey of the sexes, as men and women meet and celebrate themselves and one another.

Balance is the ability of men and women to so order their relationships as to maximize the variety and energy of their ways of being with each other. For example, it would be tragic if a woman had always to be with a man in one mode – traditionally subordinate – and the man had always to be strong and in charge. In that case, even if he were ill, he would deny it and tell his family to "clear out." Contrarily, each partner could agree it is all right to react differently, so that a strong man becomes helpless, needing a nurse, or a weak woman makes a show of strength by remaining on her feet even though quite ill, thus receiving the admiration of her family while swallowing her anger at not being "allowed" to be sick. Balance in the sexes means that each has, owns, and uses the qualities ascribed to both, and they celebrate this abundance in one another. There is no fear of being castrated or raped, no unhealthy competition for the position of top dog, and no need for the man to put the woman down in order to feel like a man, or for the woman to be absurdly careful of the man's fragile ego. Adam and Eve seek a fulfilling balance.

We are presently engaged in a dialogue in this country and in many other parts of the world in which the *focus* and *balance* elements of the man-woman encounter are the poles around which are gathering the changing identities of each sex. As women discover their needs and the needs of men in the twentieth century, they attempt to gather resources necessary for meeting those needs. Educated, articulate, talented women see no reason to accept financial dependence. In an overcrowded world, most women will not make motherhood the only significant task of their adult years. With the new freedom of the contraceptive, women are also liberated from their sexual prisons and given a new *genital* reality – they can and should enjoy sexual satisfaction and fulfillment. They can decide whether or not to bear children on the basis of their own personal data for making the choice, and not on the basis of a societal overlay regarding this decision. This separates childbearing from sexual-genital pleasure.

In the midst of these enormous changes, women are trying to focus on the ancient question of "Who am I?" It is also true for men who – faced with the "more is better" value assumptions of our culture that impose the more work, more money, more *things* merry-go-round – often find themselves depressed with jaded values and feelings and terrible bitterness.

The "Who are *we*?" question then emerges as men and women struggle for individual and corporate identity. They are asking questions that have no automatic answers, and some drive right to the roots of the ultimate meaning of man and woman: Are we different except for the organs that function for pleasure and propagation?

Any attempt to say yes to this question has to do with focus:

how else do man and woman differ? Even if we assume that men and women are custodians of certain values or human resources that are clearly designated male and female, there is no evidence to prove that these are hormonally decided. Primary and secondary sexual characteristics – genitals, breasts, hair, voice, and the like – are hormonal effects. There is no clear evidence that women are assigned moral, psychological, or emotional custodianship. Society may do that, but, as we have said, that means that man and woman are then denied certain rights more theirs as human beings than theirs as a sex. A *person* needs to be able to cry, regardless of what little boys are supposed to do. A *person* needs to show affection, to embrace and kiss, regardless of what a cold father and a warm mother might have taught. A *person* needs to cultivate his or her intuitive side regardless of the fact that women had to be intuitive because men told them they were not rational creatures and to act so would be to appear masculine. A *person* raises children regardless of what Mommie says and what Daddy does.

It is clear that being male or female is at the heart of one's identity, but we have lost much of our humanity in trying to protect our sexual roles (mother and father), our sexual property (virgins), our sexual lust (the body beautiful), and so on. A total woman concept denigrates woman if she, as *person*, is seduced while seducing her man. The total woman is half-a-person. She manages to capture and keep her man only at the price of her pride, and at the expense of her own autonomous ego. Her life is meaningful only in the catering and pandering posture of servant and sex object. It is a prostitution of all that might be called holy in personhood and an adulteration of the sexual partnership of equality. The woman's selfhood is lost in the pampering and babying of her greedy and devouring man. The assumption that her man will return the favors is an afterthought, attached as a hope or dream, but never a part of a contract between the man and woman to get each other deeply loved and cared for. Robert A. Johnson's book, *She*, tells of Amazon women who cut off a breast in order to handle the bow and arrow with greater accuracy. The opposite in a total woman complex might suggest that women grow a third breast because her man likes the other two so well. Total-woman females have slain the *animus* and survive as half-persons, and only a total man, oblivious to his *anima* or an effeminate total-woman-sort-of-male could tolerate her truckling, menial, babydoll ways. A male chauvinist stud, whose focus is total genital, or a Milquetoast sort of man who needs the total woman to inspire and erect him, will love her. Men who want a whole woman friend, partner, and lover will not.

The new focus of sexual differences may then have to do with helping each other realize and express man-in-woman and woman-in-man. Perhaps a woman's greatest gift to man is to call for his *anima* and give him a supportive environment in which to experience his own femaleness. Only a whole woman is secure enough to permit the man to express his feminine side, and only a whole man, who trusts his manhood, is free and secure enough to give expression to the feminine side of him. Of course, the opposite is true: perhaps the man's greatest gift to the woman is to call for and support the expression of her *animus*, her masculine side, and thus encourage her to be a *whole person* rather than total woman. We should be striving for a whole person concept rather than some total gender concept that leaves a man and a woman looking strained, overstated, and ridiculous in their relationship.

Perhaps, in fairness, we should say that women seem more willing to let men express their *anima* than men seem willing to let women express their *animus*. A man may be able to rise to the contest among other men and be beaten because his opponent was "a better man," but the same man may be horrified at the sight of a woman on the playing field of sports, office, or bed. She must not be assertive, strong, competitive, or initiating. Nothing is more humiliating for some men than to be beaten by a woman. Even if the woman is reassuring and supportive, the man is likely to be suspicious and jealous. He wants her off his field (unless she is his sexy cheerleader with pom-poms), out of his office (except as his playful and seductive maid), and out of his bed (other than as playboy bunny for his pleasure and satisfaction). The twin to this sort of male is the anxious man who feels he is not quite making it as a man unless he can give "his woman" an orgasm, perhaps multiple orgasms, *every* time.

Genital

Most adults desire genital union. Most of us strive for this and are incomplete and unfulfilled without it. All male-female meetings of consequence are conditioned by a fantasy, the memory, or an anticipation of genital intercourse. This does not mean that every time men and women meet, they are consciously preoccupied with genital union; but they are at least conditioned by what is imagined or experienced genitally with that person or some other.

The possibility of genital union significantly affects what transpires between a man and a woman. The person before you is not a neuter. He or she is either man or woman. That makes a difference, regardless of the conversation or the activity shared. That difference is a numinous, erotic field of woman or man generated out of the entire human experience. Central to that field is the possibility of genital union in fantasy, memory, or anticipation: if not now, sometime; if not here, somewhere; and if not with this person, then with someone.

More universally than anything else, genital intercourse fulfills man and woman. It represents symbolically and delivers substantively our deepest sense of wholeness and health. It is the ground of pleasure and the body's surest ecstasy. It is, then, not unlikely that meetings between men and women become charged in ways in which meetings with the same sex, for heterosexuals, are not. It is because quite explicitly – or buried somewhere in the psyche as the merest hint, like jasmine – there is the promise of the ultimate human bond, man and woman living in genital embrace.

In addition to foreplay and afterplay, genital union between loving adults has at least three other distinct aspects. They are *penetration, synthesis*, and *orgasm*.

1. The moment of *penetration* signals genital union, the unique conditioning fantasy in male-female meeting. It is in that moment that man convincingly crosses the threshold into woman. She welcomes him with abandon. There is an exultant *sense of arrival*. Every touch, look, word, and maneuver has led to this homecoming of the sexes. Even in the mythology of the virgin, it is the moment when girl becomes woman, boy be-

comes man, as though penetration symbolically opens the way
and sets free. It is transitional – a rite of sexual passage. More
profoundly, it is the *meeting* of man and woman.

2. *Synthesis*, if it occurs, transcends even this union. After
penetration there comes the shifting, moving, and lifting; the
warm mouth of the vagina receiving every stroke of the penis
with an intuition and a *yes* followed by the slightest inflection
of muscle; *no*, then a new turning, rolling, slipping toward synthesis, when the two become one and each the other. There is at
the center a waiting in the psychic roots of all our genital awareness for this mystical union. The man is buried in the woman.
She envelops him. They say their words, meaningless, precious,
reassuring. They lift, hover, and sail. They whimper and battle,
bathe and caress toward the melding, in the clutching, tangled
mix of fire, gasping breath, and pelvic hinging or thrusting, the
air turbulent with a sweet, riding home alone, together, one.
And the rhythm of that ride is the fine meter of all their meeting.

3. *Orgasm* is central to what our nature is about in genital intercourse. Anyone who settles for less needs to understand that
is exactly what has happened. There are exciting trips in which
"getting there is half the fun," but only half. The so-called trip is
about *arriving*. So is orgasm. Without it there is often painful
and frustrating disappointment. When lovers know what arriving is like, they will only reluctantly continue to settle for half
the fun of getting there.

We finally come down to whether or not a man and woman
can experience that most abandoned moment of all, when the
body and psyche, risking everything, explode into each other's
awareness with breathless expansion and release and with gratitude for "such a gift as this between us, for me and for you." Afterwards follows a beautiful tranquillity when the subtlest
messages of love and tenderness are exchanged, and then sleep.

There is always a danger of getting caught in the spell being
woven by those who tout orgasm as worthy of worship. Such
evangelism can be expected as we emerge from our Puritan de-
nialism and the male chauvinist imperialism that has featured
a hegemony over women. However, nature's balance simply as-
serts a genital communion between men and women in which

they should expect to achieve orgasm. When the body is allowed to move naturally and instinctively to its logical end, orgasm should occur. If this does not happen, we have blocked it.

As the social mores change and we take more seriously our sexual-genital needs and rights, men and women are paying more attention to what happens during lovemaking and intercourse. The pleasure experience and conception are clearly separate. Pleasure outlives the possibility of conception. Conception is necessary for survival of the race. This is surely also true of *pleasure*. Orgasm is intense pleasure and there need not be either the intention or possibility of conception.

The Masters and Johnson research has not only mapped the sexual-genital response, it also has called attention to the experience in ways that have caused us to accept, discuss, and improve that experience with our lover. There has been a deluge of books, magazine articles, workshops, and lectures on the subject. While most couples reject becoming sexual athletes, they are genuinely interested in how their bodies and psyches can be stimulated toward sensual, sexual, genital enrichment and gratification.

Perhaps it needs to be said that each one is responsible for his or her own orgasm. For years we heard that the man gave the woman her orgasm. This is impossible. With help from our partner, we get our own. Each person knows what needs to happen in order for orgasm to occur; so we must accept the fact that unless we know what we are about and can bring together the right feelings, no climax will occur regardless of our lover's intention for us. It is up to you to invite and create the kind of play most conducive to climax.

The ease and success of the new sex therapies testify to the body's ability to find its own way and reach its end. Without making absolute promises for universal success, we can say that it is now usually possible for healthy adults to achieve orgasm. Sexually unsatisfied men and women owe it to themselves to investigate the possibility of rectifying the condition. The odds for recovery are too good not to try.

Friends, partners, and lovers arriving at this point together in their relationship are now simply invited to create an environment in which they can best express their love and give pleasure to one another. In this giving we receive loving. While this is not a "how-to" sex manual, my suggestions to couples usually include something like this:

Although lovemaking may occur in many different places, the bedroom is where most of us expect it to happen. Let it reflect your taste at its most inviting and satisfying. Drab, cramped, and cluttered bedrooms with ironing boards, desks, sewing machines, and other foreign objects are disheartening. A dull, uninspired room is insulting to your own feelings. A cutesy "boudoir" littered with kewpie dolls, lacy pillows, knickknacks, and plastic flowers may not do much for the five senses. Dress the room to invite and stimulate.

Soft light, music, throw rugs and cushions for variety from bad beds and thin carpets, favorite pictures and fragrances, the right clothes or no clothes can enhance the event. There should be enough time uninterrupted by phones or children. Good talk, touching, bathing, and massaging with body lotions can be pleasant and fun. Women sometime complain that men do not talk and touch enough, so that women feel rushed and cheated of the closeness they desire. A variety of positions for intercourse, freedom for sexual fantasy, intimate language, and little, private games are appropriate. Time, place, and energy to feel loved and experience orgasm are the simple needs to be met. What both want is what should occur. We create our own unique play. *Find* each other and say so with talk and touch.

This experience is so important to marriage that it is hard to imagine too much preparation for lovemaking. Often our preparation for lesser events is more elaborate and consuming. Social parties are better given to neighbors than to our mates. Making love has a special priority in marriage, and it deserves our best effort. The love experience permeates the entire marriage and colors every nuance. We must protect this time together and frequently discuss how we might improve the experience. Few exchanges will have greater impact upon the quality of the marriage than this personal and intimate expression of what it means to be man and woman together.

Perhaps the most frequently reported sexual complaint today by both men and women is something called *inhibited sex-*

ual desire. It also seems to be the sex problem that people want least to admit. A dysfunction implies that at least you tried but failed for whatever reason, but inhibited sexual desire suggests that you not only did not try; you didn't even *want* to try. There is just no appetite. The reason for any appetite may be illusive or unexplainable whether for sex or other favorites, but to lose that appetite, especially if enjoying it requires another person, means we have some explaining to do. If I lose my appetite for Italian gourmet cooking and my mate is an Italian gourmet chef, I could very well have a problem somewhat larger than my capricious taste buds.

There are many reasons for the loss of desire, all the way from something as serious as a buried negative sexual history that has been triggered to simple stress and fatigue. Generalized depression, low-grade infections, side effects from prescription drugs, being overweight, and immoderate use of alcohol may also foster the problem. Even the fact that many people feel saturated by sexual material in the media and in daily conversation accounts for what some refer to as overkill. The quality of mystery is lost for the convenience of familiarity. Aggravated inhibition can mean unexpressed hostility toward one's mate, often still buried in the unconscious. Simple passivity often points to distractions: the job, children, aging parents with special needs, some temporary crisis, and so forth. Whenever the complaint is, "I really like it, but I just don't seem to be interested; it's just too much effort," something or someone has stolen the passion. Energy for sex just isn't there. Most people feel they have been robbed. Something they treasured has been lost, and they find it hard to know why, when or who's at fault. They would like it fixed, but occasionally do not even have the energy to work on it and don't know where to start.

There is only space enough here to make a few suggestions. Homework and home remedies are worth a try.

1. You must accept the condition as real and unwanted. "I do have it, and I don't want it."

2. See where your energy is being sapped. Is there something or someone that is demanding a lot of attention and effort just now? Can you reassign priorities and energy?

3. Talk with your mate openly and lovingly. Regardless of who has the problem, it now belongs to both of you. Experiment

with some options: change schedules, chores, time to be together. Take time out to get away together, even overnight, to
recover closeness. Talk about how it was when it was good. Begin again as lovers, talking, touching, playing sexually together.

4. If this fails (and do not wait too long), talk with a therapist.
Most often it is best to go together from the very first session,
because often the problem and surely the answer will involve
your mate.

However, there are times when inhibited sexual desire appears as the first shadow of death that falls across a relationship; therefore, it must be taken seriously, checked out, and
dealt with, for better or for worse. Whatever the problem, a loss
of passion is like running out of gas. The marriage may survive
on empty, but the relationship will not be going anywhere. Get
into communication with yourself, your mate, and a therapist
until it is solved.

Chapter 6

COMMUNICATION IS TALKING AND TOUCHING WITH LOVE

When marriage and family therapists ask couples why they have come to see them, the most common response seems to be, "We're having problems communicating." The books on communication proliferate daily with each author presenting some new theory or paradigm for enhancing communication between parties, whether in the private or public sector. More recently, presidents have been accused of failing to communicate to the people their dreams and goals for the nation.

Successful communication between couples means talking and touching in ways that leave each feeling loved. Since love should always be the ultimate standard of any significant exchange, love remains the final mark of good communication. Even when speech or action in itself might not at the moment appear loving, the receiver should feel loved by the lover. I heard a good friend once shout with an oath at his three-year-old, who was about to do something quite dangerous. The child was startled, but everyone felt the father's love as the child raced into his arms. The language of love might occasionally sound strange to an outsider, but lovers always know when they experience the communication as loving. Is it too much for a lover to say, "I always want you to feel loved by me?" I think not.

We must then pay attention to how we talk and touch. Even with all the guides, it is not easy to know which path is best, but we can cut through all the psycho-babble about communication by simply saying "I want to talk with you and touch you in such a way as to make you feel you are truly loved." Once we see this highest motive, we instinctively know a lot about how to talk and touch, provided we remember the balance wheel in every relationship: "Can I be me with you?" This question assumes that the person I want to be wants to be loved by you also. We are then in balance and can love ourselves and each other with care and wisdom. When we cannot reach this goal, we may then need help from a counselor. Still, the goal of getting each other loved remains at the heart of the relationship.

Instead of laying out yet another system for communication between friends, partners, and lovers, I decided to do a quick review that seems to summarize the guides to the kind of communication that should leave lovers feeling loved.

The ABC's of communication are a bit arbitrary. The alphabet is fixed and unadaptable. Still, it opens a shortcut to organizing a useful list of things to remember when talking together. So I suggest it as a checklist for both learning and reminding us of how we can talk together with love. If you can think of better associations with certain letters, make your own list of what you need to do to become an expert communicator with your lover.

ABC's of Couple Communication

Avoid Double-Think

Do not pretend to mind-read the other person. It is better to say, "Help me to understand exactly what you want" than, "Sure I understand. You're as transparent as a fishbowl."

Be Direct and Honest

Say what you mean and mean what you say. "You can count on it," is so much better than some other promise compromised with *if, maybe*, and *perhaps* used as excuses or bailouts.

Check It Out
When in doubt, check it out: "Are you saying . . . ?" "Have you been feeling . . . ?" Do you mean . . . ?"
Devalue the Behavior, Never the Person
To say, "I felt your joke was out of place," is a much more creative observation than, "You certainly managed to make a fool of yourself again."
Edit Out the "You" Messages and Insert "I" Messages
"I feel hurt when you don't call," is a simple report of your feelings in response to a certain behavior, and is a more useful communication than "You are a thoughtless jerk."
Forfeit Your Favorite Generalizations
The classics are "You always . . ." and "You never . . ." They *always* distract from the real problem, and are *never* helpful in an argument.
Give Strokes to Both of You
Statements of affirmation and support that say something like, "We can work it out together," act as steam valves and reduce the possibility of either partner using a power move.
Honor the Other's Feelings and Ideas
Even though you may disagree with them, you can respect the feelings and ideas of the other. "I can understand how you might feel that way" is better than, "That's a stupid way to react."
Instruct One Another in What You Want, Need, and Will Settle for
"Perhaps it will help if I let you know what I would like from our relationship." Not, "If you really loved me, you'd know what I want."
Judge Not
It has been said, "By their fruits you shall know them." The swiftest and most telling judgment is the one that we pass upon ourselves. Therefore, in an intimate relationship we would do best to avoid blaming and passing value judgments upon each other. In a loving relationship, it is then easier to admit our own faults and failures.
Know When to Say "No!"
If "No!" defines your autonomy and preserves your integ-

rity and self-respect, it is important to be able to say "No!" without hesitation. We begin as infants to say "No!" in an attempt to establish our self as unique and to test our power. As psychotherapist Alexander Lowen has said, "To *no* is to *know*."

Listen Carefully

The first response in dialogue is to say nothing, while listening carefully not just to the words but to the tone, inflection, volume, and the *levels of meaning* in the message that is being sent. There is no substitute in human companionship for a good listener.

Make Up Tenderly

The deep truth of this is acknowledged in the familiar sayings, "Never go to sleep angry with each other," and "Making up is so much fun." After a fight, to desert the field without reunion may leave the anger and hurt smoldering within you, and without making up they may turn your love to ashes. Learn to say "I'm sorry" and "I forgive you."

Note Body Language

Eyes, facial expressions, and body stance are critical signals that may either reinforce or contradict the verbal message. Congruence or harmony between what is "said" and what is "shown" makes the difference between strong, clear, straight *single* messages and conflicting *double* messages.

Open Up

Dialogue occurs as we develop patterns of self-disclosure and feedback, and this cannot begin until we are willing to let ourselves be known to another by opening up with our thoughts, feelings, and behavior. Are you a door or a wall?

Prevent Power Plays

Power plays are contests to see who is stronger and mostly have to do with trivia. There are many ways to break up power plays, for example, by asking, "What is really at stake here?" or "Why am I trying to hurt you?" or by just refusing to play the power game. We must be vigilant in avoiding power plays, yet patient with ourselves, for the only thing worse than power is powerlessness. Still, power plays will not achieve true power for anyone in an intimate relationship. True power in intimacy is mutual and shared.

Question All Your Assumptions

We change, circumstances change, possibilities change; therefore, to remain creative, energized, and alive to the future, we must be willing to reexamine our most cherished theories and our most coveted opinions. Assumptions should be like stepping stones, solid and firm under our feet until we have found and established the next step to be taken in our forward movement.

Risk

There is no growth without risk. Caution is wise, and recklessness is foolish. Somewhere in between is risk: really ingenious swift kicks, preferably self-administered that allow us to bet our selves on being the best we can be.

Say You're Sorry

Saying you're sorry and meaning it can save you from all sorts of evils: plastic sainthood, "the-devil-made-me-do-it" excuses, and interminable sophomoric debates. Besides, it robs your partner of one of the oldest, most tired accusations of all: "You *never* say you're sorry." Few phrases contain more pure magic than "I'm truly sorry."

Trust Your Feelings

All feelings are our friends. They tell us how we are doing in the world. They are trusted spies who report back to us on the effects of incoming messages: "What she said made you sad"; "What he did made you mad." It is imperative that we know, name, and own our feelings. They are energy. They are the gas in the car of our ideas and values. They get us down the road, unless we block, bury and suppress our feelings. Then we become depressed, immobilized, and out of gas. We may have many different feelings about any one thing. Then we must choose the best, most creative *executive* feeling, the most refined and highest octane: anger, grief, joy — whatever it takes to drive our ideas and values into the most fruitful behavior.

Unload Those Feelings Carefully

Dumping is dangerous. Many people with powerful feelings such as anger, grief, or fear often seem to be looking for a scapegoat, someone to dump them on. Intimacy cannot tolerate our bringing "home" such feelings and waiting for an excuse (or even setting up our partner) to take the rap in order that we might be free of the burden of those feelings. Dumping feelings takes the creativity of an artist. Taking a walk, doing some manual work, or being alone may better enable us later to *share* our feelings and get them out without using our intimacy as a garbage dump.

Verify Your Facts

Accusations from gossip, hunches, or circumstantial evidence are unfair and hurtful, and can even be deadly to the relationship. Feelings need facts before action. That is, they need the best reasoning of the mind handling reality. So much strife in intimacy is caused by half-truths and empty suspicions. When you get the facts, present them honestly, convincingly, and with compassion. "Gotcha" is not a game of love.

Welcome Humor

Welcome humor – applied like a salve to the error, temper tantrum, self-righteousness, or whatever has inflated us or the situation into a caricature of ourselves or reality. A Chinese proverb says "Laughter is the sound of victory." In a relationship of intimacy there can be no loser or else both are losers, so where is the victory? Laughter dissolves the enemy – ignominious pride. Learning to laugh at ourselves is a great gift to our relationships.

X-Ray Your Own Soul

Verbs beginning with an "x" are rare, but here "x-ray" is quite appropriate. We need to look for ulterior motives, buried resentments, secret reservations, and hidden jealousies. Intimacy is made fragile by undisclosed agenda and wrong judgments, and is destroyed by an empty love. Taking a good look at our inside self can help to keep us honest as we attempt to create intimacy with another human being. Be reflective. Pay attention to your own inwardness as glimpsed in dreams, fantasies and sudden insights. Keeping a journal is a proven, ancient method for maintaining the inner dialogue. Put it in writing and you will find that you are less apt to stew and get caught in obsessive thought. Using a letter-writing format is often a good way to get started. Start with "Dear ____," and see whose name appears, then write them a letter – even to God.

Yield to Wholeness

Monologues are static; dialogues are dynamic. Even in intimacy we are tempted to remain apart, to protect our hardwon individuality, and turn the other into an object. Nature seeks wholeness, in some forms even regrowing lost parts, and in everything striving for wholeness, a gestalt, salvation. With such an energy at work in the universe and in us, to *yield* is to release ourselves to the healing forces at work all about us, bringing us into harmony and health. Health means wholeness.

Zero in on Love

Feeling loved by the other is the highest value in the intimacy of couples. It is therefore the task of each to monitor what the other needs in order to feel loved, and try to enable that loving to happen. For a person to feel loved may mean for the other to support a job or task rather than doing the loving himself or herself. For example, if a person needs to get away alone for a few days, supporting that trip with help and encouragement makes the other feel loved. It is very important that couples talk and touch regularly in order to know how to help the other to feel loved. For if you do not feel it, it is not working, no matter how much you believe or know you are loved. Love is an abstract noun. Loving is active and real.

Chapter 7

LOVE, WORK, AND PLAY: CELEBRATING LIFE TOGETHER

When Sigmund Freud was asked the meaning of life, he replied, "Lieben und arbeiten," love and work. Although there is evidence of splendid humor and wit in Freud, he was a citizen of the serious and reserved Victorian age in which he lived, and might be forgiven for not including the third dimension of a whole life: play. Without the spirit of play, we are lost.

After childhood we turn play into work with sweat and no-pain-no-gain exercise. Yet, we can find in the first three chapters of our Judeo-Christian Scriptures at least the hint of a playful spirit, which may be helpful for those of us also raised with a Puritan work ethic in the shadows of the post-Victorian era. In the story of Genesis, we discover God's *love* for his creation and assume a loving Adam and Eve. There is the birth of intimacy. We can also find God at *work* in creation, commanding us to work, and thereby enabling us to become co-creators with him. With a bit of poetic license, we can find celebration, perhaps even *play*, in God's spirit of pleasure and delight with his work as he exclaims, "It is good!" at the end of the day.

When couples struggle with the currencies of time, energy and money, I ask them to draw three interlocking circles that represent in relative size the importance of love, work, and play in their marriage. Some draw circles that barely touch or float freely and are of disproportionate size. For most, work is the largest circle, with love and play attached like Mickey Mouse ears. But if they draw integrated circles of equal size and balance, they create the figure below.

Before you proceed, why don't you draw your own pattern to show how you see your own marriage. Then later after your mate has drawn one also, you may decide to discuss your drawings. Such talk can be quite revealing and helpful.

A glance at the figure quickly suggests obvious dynamics that make for a creative use of this perspective. As they interlock, they interact.

For example, we must work at love as with a garden, and we should love our work. To play with those ideas may cause us to ask how working on our loving might be more creative. Such a discussion could bring us to examine our vocation as well as our own work together on the relationship, especially regarding feelings and commitment.

We must often work at play when we are learning a new way to play, such as dancing, playing a sport, or making love, before we can simply relax and enjoy what we have learned to do. We must also be able to play at our work, since that is usually when we are most creative. The playful dance of the imagination brings inventiveness to our work, expanding its dimensions and keeping it from becoming stale.

Finally, we should love to play for the refreshment and delight of it. We must also be able to play at love if it is to be spontaneous and full of the abandon we knew in childhood by simply enjoying our bodies.

It might be helpful to discuss how three interlocking circles with arrows pointing both ways between each two circles could help us be more intimate, creative, and celebrative as friends, partners, and lovers. Then focus on the center or the eye where these great movements of life synthesize. When is your deepest moment of intimacy both creative and celebrative? One couple who postponed having a baby were devastated when the husband was sent to Viet Nam. Unlike many couples in such situations who, fearing the worst, try to begin a pregnancy before the husband leaves, this couple decided to wait until he returned, using that dream as a seed of hope and a prayer for protection. When he came home, they arranged to meet at a cabin in Colorado that was special to them and agreed not to use birth control. The wife later said, "I knew I was pregnant at our first intercourse. We simply exploded with each other."

When I am working with couples or individuals who are stuck with an experience or feeling I often try to help them focus so they can move on by finding the word that best describes where they are. Then I suggest they look for additional words, synonyms, that further define or expand that trigger word, so that they master it and take control.

Love

Let's begin with the word *love*. I choose *life* as the defining word beginning with "L." Love is an abstract word, one which is sometimes hard to grasp. But when I think of love as life, then I have a sense of being able to do something with myself in my relationship with my wife, family, friends, and my God in a loving way that becomes for me the essence of being alive. Life is symbolized by love, and love becomes the moving force of my life. So I say, "How am I going to stay alive?" By breathing. "How am I going to live?" By loving. Loving is what life is all about. Everything else inspires and encourages my loving.

Recent research on cocaine addicts gives us an interesting profile. Most heavy users of cocaine tend to be ambitious, self-centered men who lack the capacity for intimacy with a woman.

Coke, it is said, seems to promise what many seek in life: satisfaction, fulfillment, joy, and even intense ecstasy, but it delivers death. Cocaine is seen, then, as a substitute for women. If we are trying to turn life into a love experience, when we cannot do it, life turns barren and we turn to the next closest thing.

What word would you choose for the letter "L"? How would you illustrate how love and life are so bound together?

Oneness is the word I chose to represent the letter "O." In recent years there has been some resistance to the idea of oneness in marriage. To many, the thought of two becoming one is too confining. It implies a loss of autonomy. According to Plato, humans were originally composed of a male and a female half. Then the gods split that creature into two, and we were set free in the world to search for our other half. Other Greeks had an even stranger notion of male/female wholeness. They believed that at one time males and females were like eagles, one with a loop on one side where the wing belonged and the other with a hook. They paired by finding each other, hooking up this way, and flying away. Once again, this suggests the desire to find our soul mate, to connect and bond into wholeness. Representing our need to believe in finding that one person for whom we were *intended*, this idea is part of the more accepted idea of *realizing our own true self*, arriving at our personal sense of *wholeness*.

I shall never forget the stark statement a man made at the beginning of our first session in my office: "When I married my wife, we became less instead of more." Then he paused and looked at me as though he had just said it all.

Even if we are vigilant in protecting each other's autonomy, to respect our differences and uniqueness, our need to feel separate, there is still the longing for union, for a fusion that is ancient and profound. But the question is how can we acknowledge that yearning without sacrificing the singleness that is so essential for our own health and that of the marriage?

In Genesis we read: "Therefore a man leaves his father and his mother, and clings to his wife, and they become one flesh (2:24, NRSV)." Why? How? I can only understand it as a metaphor. On the continuum toward intimacy, I value the concept of being one's own person. Yet, I have also used the question, Can I be me with you? as the balance between being single and being married, the part and the whole, as I have tried to respect the individual and insist that connecting is the *sine qua non* in a great love.

The concept of oneness in marriage is a cry of the soul, not unlike the cry for God. It is a longing, an ineffable prayer at the core which hints at all our desire for a mythic union where all things come together in a great meld that implies ultimate belonging and even perfection. I recall during the days of our brief engagement how right it seemed that Dian and I had found each other. I best glimpsed this in a fleeting moment during an embrace, when the only way to express it was my sense of how well we *fit* in as many aspects of togetherness as I could imagine, most of which lay yet ahead since we hardly knew each other at the time.

Since these often come only as moments, hints at a depth in us, as the eternal *now*, we must be on the alert for these glimpses of a sense of oneness, which are given serendipitously. However, these gifts are rare and may come when we are not expecting them. What else can we do? We can enter into environments with our mate where we may expect such a visitation: a holy place, a place in nature, an underwater place where we swim to view that world together, or listening to music, planting a garden, writing a poem together with each composing a line at a time, finger painting, creating one picture together – all experiences that promise the possibility of the grand union.

Talk together about your need for oneness. Perhaps you do not feel this desire, but if your mate does, he or she may experience a great loss if it is seldom or never satisfied. For many, to arrive at such a moment is best expressed not as mutual sexual orgasm but as the great orgasm of the soul. Wonder about it. Look for it. But if you find it, don't try to capture and retain it or it just may go flat like a child's balloon the day after the party.

The word for "V" is *vows*. I cannot imagine a great love without vows. These also have depreciated in the last decade or so: "I am what I am, I do what I do, I make no promises." Yet, we know that we cannot have any structure, system, or significant, long-term relationship without promises. "Will you be here forever, tomorrow, or for the next five minutes?" We must *know* in order to do life with any continuity or consistency.

It is with the promise that all things are ordered, made sense of. It is the promise that drives us on even when we're in a place that tempts us to stay.

Yes, you say, but promises get broken. You are right, and the necessity of the promise may be only proved as some are broken, but they are not *made* to be broken. They only break when we are careless or we allow other promises to supersede them. I recall a woman in therapy once whose first husband had left her with two children. She met and married a second man who was good to her children, but decided he wanted one of his own with her. She consented and after five years he announced that he felt trapped and wanted out. She came to me when yet a third man wanted to marry her. He too was good with her children. He had never been married and had no children of his own. She was afraid to bring up her worst fear. She waited. Then one night he said, "I know your history with men and children, but I love you so much I can't imagine not having a child with you." She burst into tears, and called me for an appointment the next day. She said, "When I was very young I thought the worst fate imaginable was boredom, and I did everything I could not to get tied down. Then it began to happen." She told me her story about men and children, concluding, "There is some predictability that is not boring." She paused, then asked, "What can I do? I'm afraid to risk it."

All she could do was to make herself a promise that this would be her last marriage, and with it that she and her new husband would promise to stay in touch every day, to love and care and cherish, and if it chanced that they hit trouble, to seek help immediately. After weeks of premarital work, they married and I believe they always will remain married. But it was her one promise to herself that enabled her to take the risk again: "This one will be the last." Sometimes it is the promise to ourselves that is the hardest to keep, but it may be the only one we will finally trust. If so, it is better to go with that one than not to go at all. Vows may be a little like the thorns we must respect in order to gather the rose.

I have been moved over the years to see so many couples "say their vows" again after their marriage has sustained some terrible blow and survived. Occasionally there is even a new set of rings and a honeymoon, but the vows seem essential for establishing the roots and again going down to the deep waters that feed the soul of the covenant.

The phrase "promises to keep" seems redundant. Promises *are* for keeps. Yet, there is no virtue in just the keeping. The promise is not about itself, but something beyond it: "I promise to love you, never to leave you." These are mere words. The promise, the vows, point beyond themselves to the relationship. It is a way of accenting the value and the commitment of that relationship. To vow to love means that I vow to be loving, to act loving, to make love happen, and not merely to vow. "Promises kept" is a great farewell to a great relationship provided only that the relationship itself was daily full of promise. It is not enough to say, "Well, at least we stayed married." Those words are as bleak as a tomb. Vows are no holier than the health of the wholeness to which we aspire. Promise, then love and work and play, making good your words with today's gifts and tomorrow may very well take care of itself.

Finally, we are led to the "E" word: I chose *eternal*. In the great vows of marriage we touch the eternal. The vows are intended to last forever, not until we get tired or bored or the money runs out. No one starts that way toward a great love. Since time is one of the standards by which we measure anything of value, it is a special way to measure marriage, not simply for longevity, but because it implies value.

Valuing is at the heart of the great questions of life: "Who am I?" "What do I want?" and "What will I give for it?" We are in some profound respect only energy and time. As money is used to express value, so is the amount of energy expended a way of telling the value of a thing. If we spend too much money or energy we feel ripped off. A waste of time has been called a "sin" by those who used the idea of sin to indicate how precious time really is. When people ask if I think counseling will help, I can only say that I promise them my best energy for an hour of my life in exchange for my fee. That seems like a lot to me only because I can reckon how much my energy and time mean to me.

Hence, promising to do something until my death represents an enormous commitment, and to cut that short would mean that a great tragedy had occurred in that every expectation had either been short-sighted at the beginning or that some unsuspected power had invaded the field and destroyed my fondest hope and best effort. Time stops for that promise, and the death would necessarily be viewed as premature and, thus, as at a child's death, most tragic in light of the dream. Hence, when I promise, "Until death us do part," I enter into a valuing that can only be expressed in reference to my life or, more specifically, to my death, when time ceases for me on this earth. I can promise no more. Yet, the question of time is so persistent that when Jesus was asked who a wife of many husbands might belong to in heaven, he didn't even attempt to extend the time line into some absolute eternity. He simply said marriage does not occur there. Period. Whatever one believes about all of that, time indeed is an ultimate criterion for assigning value. When I say "until death," I have said it all. Regardless of the extenuating circumstances that may disrupt our journey and bring the marriage "early" to its death, we *start* with *forever*. We cannot ignore the calendar as a way of measuring *and* valuing.

One of the most inspirational stories I know comes from Joseph Fletcher's book *Situation Ethics*. He tells of a German woman, Mrs. Bergmeier, who, as the Allies moved across Europe while the Russians reached toward Berlin, was captured by the Russians. She was taken to Russia and put in a prison camp. After a time she learned through the underground that her husband had returned from the war to their village, as had her two children. All were alive and healthy. One of the ways a prisoner could get out of the camp was to become pregnant. What do you think Mrs. Bergmeier did? She found a willing guard. Soon she was summarily expelled and told to go fend for herself. Pregnant and with no help except what she could beg with her broken Russian, she slowly made her way home. Months later she and her family stood before their Lutheran minister and had that little infant son, fathered by the Russian guard, baptized. Later, she said to Dr. Fletcher, who interviewed them personally, "That child is loved by all of us like no child ever was. He brought us home." That is doing life together, all of it! Not an affronted moralist saying, "Oh, I could never do a thing like that!" but a life partner saying, "I will give birth to life to be with you again, even alien life that we will make our own." Forever!

Work

Alice Litkins, a German novelist, said a marvelous thing about love and work: "Where love is lacking, work becomes a substitute, and where work is lacking, love becomes an opiate."

I don't know a more telling truth about the interaction of those two experiences. I remember a man I counseled years ago, an attorney who hated his work, who said in our first session, "When I walk out of my house in the morning, I'm a single man. I think single, feel single, and act single as much as I can all day long. And when I go home at night I am a married man with three kids. You've got to help me."

When work is lacking, love or sex becomes an opiate. This man is addicted. His life is about the next seduction. That is all that can really focus his life and give him satisfaction. That's when he feels most like a man. Yet, he is miserable.

Now, as we move from *love* to *work*, we do not leave love behind. It is important to remember the natural affinity these two experiences have for each other, as Litkins says and as the young lawyer suggests in his agony.

When I considered words for *work*, the "W" suggested *worth* as a key to understanding the meaning of work in our lives. Since we are identified, often defined, by what we do for a living, our work must have worth, not just for us but for our world. Sometimes we can justify our work only in terms of money. But since we spend so much of our lives at it, our work needs to have value in itself. Also, we should gain a further sense of worth because we do it. Our work is worth-y of being done, and in doing it we too are made to feel worth-y of its calling.

Of the first – the worth of our work – the American journalist and critic, Alexander Woollcott, said, "The worst sin of all is to do well that which should not be done at all." The Nazis epitomized this idea as they became expert at eliminating mass populations. Clients often tell me how trapped they feel because of security needs, longevity, or other extenuating circumstances. A man recently said, "You know, I do my job really well, but I hate it. I cannot imagine why anyone would buy our product. I wouldn't own one myself, yet I spend eight hours a day trying to make it better than our competition, better than my boss did before I got his job, and even better than the jerk that will replace me. I want it to be perfect, and it disgusts me. I don't have a job. It's got me."

Some work deepens our sense of self-worth just because we do it. I know teachers, ministers, nurses, mental health professionals, and others who feel ennobled by their vocation. It is indeed a "calling" that sets them on the course of their career.

They feel they serve the needs of others, often at personal sacrifice, in order to make their lives a little better. Many believe that God called them to their work, and even though they may feel unworthy, they are given worth by taking up the work. Martin Luther said that the lowliest scrubwoman's work was on a par with a priest at the altar if she believed that she, too, served God and dedicated her work "to the glory of God." One must be a believer to redeem his or her work that way.

Yet, not everyone can summon such a redeeming religious faith. Others simply see a need and are glad to be accepted as part of a special team. These people often excel in their work, enlivened by a deep sense of purposefulness that others who simply "take the job" do not feel. It is especially hard in a dehumanizing environment where people are treated merely as replaceable parts with serial numbers, in which any "body" could be filling the slot.

Problems arise when our work is fractional and we are not connected to the whole product, or when the work seems unnecessary, or senseless, or not congruent with our values. While many people simply go numb at work and put in their time, others feel profoundly discounted by it. A teacher said to me when she resigned after twenty-three years of award-winning classroom work: "Nobody cares — not the board or the superintendent or the principal or the parents or the students. Why should I? It is no longer the high calling it was for me when I was a young woman. I wake up in tears five days a week."

If people feel lucky to have any job at all, it is hard to give much thought to the worthiness of the work, but in a culture that touts family values and religious faith, we should try to help people who hate their work to somehow redeem it, so that they may engage in it with pride. Or we should help them to move in a new direction, as this teacher knew she had to do.

In marriage, the worthiness of our work can affect our relationship. In some ways we are extensions of our work, and our mate may feel that in our work we are also extensions of him or her. Therefore, how we feel about our work reflects on us as well as our mate. I have gathered some questions that may help review how we feel about our jobs as well as how we experience the whole work sphere together. Talk through these and see how the worth-i-ness of work affects your relationship. What needs more "work" in order to enhance the work experience of your marriage?

How do I describe what I do for a living?

How do I feel when asked about my work?

Am I compromised by my work?

Would I want a child of mine to do my kind of work?

Is my work so satisfying that if I did not need the money, I would still want to do that kind of work?

How do you, my mate, feel about my work?

What are the positive and negative contributions of my work to our relationship?

Is there something I can do to enhance the worthiness of my work?

Finally, do I work in our home with pride and a sense that somehow what I do with you for us is the most special, even noble, labor of all? How can my efforts be improved so that the work of our home is a labor of love?

There were many "O" words to choose from as I contemplated *work*, from *opportunity* to *obligation* to *occupation*, but I chose *option*, because it means "choices," which is the very heart of autonomy. I choose my work and it chooses me. Also, within the doing of my work I remain alert for choices, because the ability to choose these keeps my work alive for me. Indeed, my work may remain a live option for me because it affords choices that keep a creative tension between me and my product.

The positive implications of making the choice of our life's work are the same in a good marriage. When each chooses the other, the knot is strong. If one only feels chosen, but is not choosing, it is unbalanced; it is not a good knot. Jesus says of his followers that many are called but few are chosen, implying that to be chosen is "choice," to be preferred. It is sad to hear someone say, "I feel that I love my mate more than she loves me." Each needs to feel chosen, not just reacted to in a measured way or indulged. I have a colleague who speaks of his stepdaughter as his "chosen daughter."

As we use the word "choice" to suggest quality so it is to be chosen: "You are chosen, choice, unique." It is one thing to choose a mate. It is quite another to make your mate feel that he or she is choice, special. When the love is unbalanced, it is hard to feel special. When you feel chosen, you know you are choice, for who would choose what is less than the best? Of all my options, I chose you!

A second reason I picked *options* as a key word in *work* has more to do with choices *within* the work. More and more home industries are developing because people want options of time, place, and energy. Jobs are given options with the availability of computers and FAX machines. Single parents need options regarding schedules and time off. To have optimum choice in all matters of our work is a great victory for autonomy and human dignity. I have always kept evening and Saturday hours for clients who could not get away from their jobs during regular working hours. Yet, lately I find that all of that is changing. People work irregular hours, or have more options about time, even if it means getting away from their jobs each week for months to see me. "Just so I get the work done," many will say. Everything – from dress codes to time and place – is more negotiable. This opens up the work situation and makes us feel we can breathe. We have choices.

The most important considerations regarding options still have to do with how work is experienced by and in the intimate relationship of the couple. The schedule, stress, challenge, compensation and the very character of the work affect the quality of the relationship. The working formula for the couple is similar to the one most people use regarding sex: whatever both agree to is fine. Yet, since work is one of the major arenas of life, the more options we have, the more likely we are to find happy solutions to work problems within the marriage. Rigidity makes the relationship brittle.

Recently in a session, a young husband who had been laid off from his job in the automotive industry, said, "Well, the last thing I need is for the guys to call me a househusband." His response to that fear was not to do housework and not to be seen driving their daughter to school even though he did not now have to leave home early in the morning. He would share chores as he had before, but he was not about to take on his wife's also. So what did he do? He played golf and fished. For the first time in their marriage, his wife felt taken advantage of.

In a great love, the work options must be as open as possible, so that the enormous energy of work may be economically handled by the couple and for the couple and not *just* for a boss or money or some stereotypical notion of man's work and woman's work. It is refreshing to swap jobs, to break up the routines of how and when, and in every way keep those labor-intensive tasks of the relationship and home as light and upbeat as possible. One couple suddenly realized that they did not have to use Saturday morning to clean and do chores when they had evenings that were often spent watching TV programs that were mostly unsatisfying. So on Saturday mornings they began going to the farmer's market, where they met new friends and had a different experience than they had anywhere else in their lives.

Feeling that you have options is a state of mind. It is the life-and-death trigger in addictions, depression, and other illnesses. Margaret Mead said that a depressed person is someone who believes he or she has run out of options. An addict can no longer choose. Among couples, options mean opportunity.

The "R" word I chose in *work* is *reward*. When I was completing my sixteen-month tour of duty as a chaplain in Korea, a senior chaplain tried to convince me to remain in the regular army. He cited the pay, benefits, travel, and retirement as inducements. "Besides," he said, "with frequent reassignments you get to start over every couple of years in the sermon barrel." We laughed together at those prospects, he with humor and I with terror. Although I never regretted my time in the service, even in Korea, where I learned a great deal about myself and the ministry, especially with men and women in crisis, I knew that what I wanted to do with my life had more to do with seminary teaching and counseling than administering chapel programs. Besides, my wife, who was an army brat, was yearning to settle down, or at least have more options about where we would live and when we would move. The rewards of a military career were considerable and not to be dismissed out of hand, but they just were not the rewards we had in mind at the time.

The rewards of work are both tangible and intangible. The tangible ones are like gas in our car. The intangible ones are like the air we breathe: they give meaning to our lives beyond compensation. For some, work, like virtue, is said to be its own reward. Over the years, the older generation often berated the youth who do not seem to value work with: "You should have lived during the Depression, then you'd know how lucky you are to have any job at all." Many men committed suicide when they lost their jobs. To seek work was a matter of pride. To be fired was a loss of dignity. Work took on a transcendence. When a man "found work" it was an occasion for celebration. Work itself was a reward. Occasionally one still sees this phenomenon, especially in depressed areas of the country where the job structure of the community is changing as in Detroit or smaller one-industry towns that have lost their trade to conglomerates.

In marriage, the rewards of work should be clearly understood as part of the contribution one makes to the general welfare of the couple. If the earnings are different, the meaning of that difference should be understood and accepted by both parties. Only then will difference not become inequity, something for one to throw up to the other. Again, whatever both agree to is fine. But if one is lazy, refuses to grow and change, is afraid to ask for a raise, or demands an unfair freedom to do odd jobs or work part time, problems in the marriage are likely to arise that can be quite destructive.

As I have said elsewhere, one must not feel taken advantage of if the partnership is to survive. Four times as many working mothers spend time away from their jobs because of child-related problems as do fathers. It is no surprise that women complain of clear inequities in relationships. Since money and sex remain as two of the great standards of a marriage against which much of the rest of the relationship is weighed, both mates must understand and accept the *reason* for the inequity and not let it invade the intimacy between them. Whatever happens, taunting of the *my* money and *your* money kind can be vicious and should be avoided at all costs. "My job is more important than your job" can also diminish love's erotic response.

All rewards of work should at some level be shareable. The more they are, the better, because these become causes for continued celebration when the satisfactions of work feed the marriage. A husband said, "I didn't care what she did with our money until I found out that her TV preacher was a crook." But it was a matter of faith for the wife, and it was hard for her to appreciate his contempt for someone whose ministry she felt had blessed her. This difference of opinion created enormous stress in their relationship, and was not even solved when the preacher was hauled off to prison. She still believed, but he closed the bank account. A solution began when he agreed to find another TV ministry that they could both support with their giving. This brought him out of an indifference to the spiritual area of his wife's life, and caused him to begin to reflect on his own faith. Their conversations finally got them out of the house on Sunday to a neighborhood church that gave them much more than what he called her "TV Joy-Boy." The rewards of work again became shareable.

The words for the "K" in *work* came briefly and without much persuasion. I considered *know* as we should know our work like a knowing intimacy, but that seemed obvious. I even considered the taunt attributed to Truman: "If you can't stand the heat, get out of the *kitchen*," as a "K" word suggesting that we should do our work without blaming or complaining, a sentiment I hear often in therapy when one partner doesn't want to talk at dinner because the other is constantly complaining without doing anything about the situation. But that was only one negative piece of the problems surrounding work in the marriage, so I decided on *killer*, feeling deeply that whatever a job may be, it must not be a killer.

In the face of work-related stress, surely protection from one's work is a must. There are two ways for work to kill you: when it is in fact packed with unmitigated stress or latent peril like coal mining or even low-level toxic exposure, and when it is the whole meaning of your life and you are required to give it up. Some die right after retirement or other great loss, such as prestige, public office, or health. If your work is your life, when you lose it, you lose your life.

When I was a young regimental chaplain at Fort Jackson, S.C., in 1954, I counseled many young officers and their wives, who were unable to get pregnant. This infantry training regiment was on rigorous duty. The training team was often working seven days a week for as many as sixteen hours a day. The training was a killer, as was the war in which many of the young recruits would go to Korea and be back in front of me in caskets before the next recruits finished their sixteen-week cycle. We lost more than 50,000 troops in Korea. When the sperm count was found to be low among the newly married training officers, we decided that it was due to their stressful duty. So a relief cycle was established in order that the men could have lighter work days and an occasional long weekend. Their sperm counts then rose and their wives became pregnant. The work was literally killing a couple's chance to start a family.

There is distress that can kill you and *eu-stress* that can inspire you, the Greek prefix *eu* meaning good as in eulogize, to say a good word. Arnold Toynbee writes of herring fishermen in the North Sea. Years ago they found their fish were sluggish when kept in the boat's hold for weeks at sea, and hence brought a poor price at market. What to do? They began putting a few catfish in with the herring to keep them moving. Sometimes to have the mortgage of your dream home, or college costs for a deserving son or daughter, or even medical bills for someone you cherish nibbling at your heels can be *eu-stress* that keeps us working for the ones we love. In such cases our spirits soar as we meet the challenge and reach our goals, even if the going gets rough at times.

Often, one sign of a weakening marriage is deeper investment of time and energy in work as a place to hide or one place we feel certain to get something accomplished. But just as often, perhaps even more so, I see marriages suffering from emotional starvation because the killer master has made a slave of its worker. I have from time to time even heard a spouse say, "Oh, everybody says he's going to work himself to death." Then she adds, "I know it's killing us," meaning the family. So, even if we love our work and get great joy and energy from it, that same rewarding work may be destroying everything else we hold dear.

Perhaps now would be a good time to reflect: Is there any way that my work could be called a killer? If so, how does it kill? Whom is it killing? What can I/we do to stop the killing? And perhaps the most troubling question of all, how far gone am I? How far gone are we? In this day when articles, books and workshops on stress are multiplying daily and work is most often seen as the culprit, the "K" word in describing *work* is a must. Talk about your work with those who suffer with you. Discuss change if change is due. For most of us, work is like fire; managed it is a great servant but uncontrolled, a potential holocaust.

Before we move on, examine the cross-currents between love and work. How might it be said that you love your work and devotedly work at love? What are the rewards and the dangers in either? Then, as we make the transition now to *play*, consider how we need to play at our work to make it less boring and more creative, and how we may need to work more at our play so it can be more relaxing and fulfilling, such as learning a new sport, how to plan a musical instrument, or a new dance. We work at play in order to be able to play at play so that it may nurture us.

Play

The third word we're going to consider is *play*. It comes from the Greek *pleien* and means "to dance." As we play through the four words chosen to describe play, keep the root meaning of dance in mind as a metaphor for understanding some of the finer aspects of play. I think immediately of Nikos Kazantzakis's fictional hero, Zorba, in the novel *Zorba the Greek* who was a tireless dancer and lover, and while he artfully avoided work, knew how to play. When the book and movie were popular, I was amused at how frequently the title was misquoted as *Zorba the Great*. While it is easy enough to transpose *Greek* and *Great*, I felt it was our instinct for his greatness of spirit that unconsciously fed the error and made us want to celebrate the Zorba in each of us.

Some years ago John Huizinga wrote his searching study of the play element in culture titled *Homo Ludem*, a Latin title for *Man the Player*, as a further elaboration of metaphors from *homo sapiens*, man the thinker and *homo faber*, man the maker. Huzinga's book is a cornucopia of profound and interesting observations about play. He says, "You can deny, if you like, nearly all abstractions: justice, beauty, truth, goodness, mind, God. You can deny seriousness, but not play." He believes that play permeates all great archetypal activities of the human experience. Play is everywhere in living creation. It simply happens in all of nature and we are delighted with it. We even speak of the "play of moonlight upon the water." We are amused, moved, fascinated, and disturbed by the presence of play in our lives. It is in language, arts, religion, mythology, poetry, ritual, and games. It represents our apprehension of rhythm, harmony, balance, and beauty. Play is the fundamental dance of the spirit. Hence, we must include it as one of the three great arenas of being and living. It cries out for its own sphere, its own playing field, its own reality.

The "P" word I chose is *pleasure*, among so many one of the obvious. There are few things that give human beings more pleasure than the movement of the body. Dance may have been our first religious ceremony, our first gift to the gods. Certainly the Bible makes a point of David's dancing before Yahweh, even then late in our religious evolution. In 1923, the British psychologist and writer, Havelock Ellis, wrote what is now a classic, *The Dance of Life*, in which he used the dance to symbolize the great rhythm of the universe and as archetypal as a symbol of the human experience.

When play is not pleasure it becomes one of the truly great absurdities. When Dian and I were living in the officers' housing after I returned from Korea, one of the pastimes for couples was to get together to play bridge. Certain officers developed a reputation for their style of playing. Some were deeply reflective and serious, watching the play like hawks and remembering every card played. They were strategists. They played as in that great oxymoron, "war games," which meant it was all work and keeping score. If they liked you, they might even teach you a trick or two. If you were playing at less than masters' level, forget it. The room was always like a tomb, with only the ice in the cold drinks rattling like old bones. At the opposite end of the spectrum from these generals was the man who was also a master player, but was no longer in the war room thinking and strategizing. The battle was joined. He was at war! He began tough and scrappy, but soon turned cruel and cold-blooded with his taunting jabs. Only those who enjoyed hand-to-hand combat played with him. There was in fact no play, no pleasure, and the only dance was the *danse macabre*. All of us have seen these types. Not only their play but their whole life might be called the "dance of death." Their only pleasure is in winning. Intimidation is their style. If you consent to play with such persons, the game is a sadomasochistic blood-letting. Occasionally, perhaps typically, the wife becomes a victim, and you can see immediately right through the walls into their intimacy, and its face is death. Fortunately, there were many other couples with whom we had wonderful experiences simply playing a game and enjoying each other's company.

Reminding us to keep play pleasurable sounds like a redundancy. It is not. In fact, my experience leads me to say that it may very well be the hardest thing to accomplish in play. We often get to it late when we are weary and carry though only because "we promised." Or we have to be good at it, then better (improving our game), then perfect, as play is magically turned into work with coaches and paraphernalia.

As I suggested earlier, play can be enhanced with the work of practice until we are good enough to enjoy it. Still, I know men who go out to play golf, and the result is anything but play. They may leave a perfectly nice office with no pain or sweat, don their cleats and clubs, and soon are addressing that little ball with every scurrilous epithet you can imagine along with a few new ones. My brother, who is quite good at the game, laughingly says, "It's a killer, but somebody has just got to get out there and beat those little golf balls back into their holes where they belong."

I am well aware of the therapeutic value ascribed to much of the effort of games, especially in the hitting, grunting, stretching, and exploding with expletives. I also know that the no-pain-no-gain concept of exercise has recently come under a lot of criticism. I know that when I ask people to write down synonyms for pleasure they almost never use the same words they select to describe pain. It is only as we try to justify the pain that is associated with certain pleasurable activities that we find the same vocabulary describing both.

Even if there is a thin line between pain and pleasure as heard in the line, "It hurts so good," I still believe that we should attempt to keep play in the pleasure zone, not only for ourselves but for those who try to play with us. A complaint I frequently hear from women regarding their lover husbands goes like this: "He's rough. He hurts me. I've tried to show him what feels pleasurable in foreplay, but he grabs and pinches and even bites. It gets so bad that sometimes I cry out. So we are doing it less and less. It's just not that much fun sometimes." A suggestion that sex therapists use perhaps more than any other is, "Learn to *pleasure* one another." So we agree that one person's passion may be another's poison. All the more reason for us to keep play pleasurable in the intimacy of lovers, if we truly want our partner to feel loved.

Our "L" word is *leisure* as we continue to play through the synonyms of words suggested by the letters of play, the third arena in the celebration of life. Our word, leisure, comes from an Old French word which means "permission," which might suggest to us the idea: "I am free to play. I have given myself that permission."

Some years ago I worked with a woman who said that she and her husband were quite troubled because she did not experience orgasm during their lovemaking. They had been married six years and had "tried everything." She had seen her gynecologist who had pronounced her to be in good physical health, but had suggested therapy. Early in the second session I asked if she would be willing to try a fantasy. After a little explanation, she agreed to try. I then asked her to close her eyes and picture what she would consider a typical sexual experience with her husband, nothing intense, just a survey of the details as through the eye of a camera. She was not to describe the event, but to figure out why she would not let herself play when they were making love. That did it. After only a few seconds into the fantasy, she heard her mother's voice saying, "You can't play until you have finished your work." In tears with her eyes open she told how after her father died her mother had to work hard to support the family of three girls. As the oldest, it was my client's job to keep house, which meant that on Saturday mornings she and her sisters had to clean before they could go out to play. Her mother worked a second job on Saturday and my client, then at age 11, had her young hands full at home. So, as a young wife, she now lay in bed thinking of all the things left undone. She was a workaholic and would not let herself play.

Leisure means permission. Not abandon, having fun, or goofing off. It means a gift to yourself. Once more, we are back to the idea of autonomy, being in charge of yourself and your life. Perhaps the best reinforcing example again has to do with sexual problems, most of which begin with anxiety about performance (work). The cure for performance problems begins by removing the expectations, the command element, and giving ourselves "permission to play in a leisurely manner." The leisure to play together is a time we decide upon and has more to do with *taking* that time than what we do with it. So, if we are asked to define leisure-time it does not have to do so much with what we do or don't do, as with our decision to permit us to take that time. The word describes an act of will rather than a kind of experience. Only when we lay claim to our authority can we truly experience the kind of letting go that permission rewards. Since many leisure-time activities require a permit, perhaps that granting of power will be our first step toward a new and liberating leisure that can leave us truly refreshed and recreated. With that permit, we can allow things to happen.

The word beginning with "A" is somewhat more obscure. I chose *aesthetic*, beautiful. I decided that play should have a sense of aesthetics about it. If we are going to talk about great love and great work and great play, loving, working, and playing with a character of greatness must indeed have about it an element of beauty, a sense of balance, form, symmetry, and rhythm. It should be beautiful like a dance.

We have a home movie of our daughter, Jennifer, when she was a little girl. I was running the camera on Christmas night as the children were saying goodnight to the tree. There was music and suddenly Jennifer began dancing around the living room. Now we have this lovely dance of a five-year-old, who never had a lesson before that night, simply letting her overflowing heart move her body beautifully. How we cherish that film!

Play needs to have some consciousness of its own form and rhythm. There's that wonderful quote from Albert Einstein, who said that there were many theories of relativity from which to choose, but he chose the one he gave us simply because it was *the most beautiful*. Perhaps only a poet-physicist could adequately explain what he meant, but at least we know that his theory appealed to his deepest instinct for the aesthetic in the universe.

If, as some believe, there is an art impulse in human beings, and if the creative spirit is most aroused in play, then it is likely that when we are truly at play, the sense of it – the sight, sound and feel of it – will touch us in ways that make us feel whole and "in sync" with the universe, even if we are neither aware of it nor would describe it that way.

Early in western civilization, Aristotle in his *Poetics* said that the properties of beauty are order, symmetry, and definiteness. I especially like that last adjective, *definiteness*, suggesting precision, clarity, boundaries. The beautiful also has a rationality about it. Music is beautiful *and* rational, perhaps each because of the other. Hence, at play we may be led instinctively by beauty's hand to move and speak with a natural current of grace, and in so doing take our play to a further distance of charm, delight, and indelibility: "I shall never forget how absolutely beautiful you were doing that, and you never even knew it." Watch a football runner moving instinctively like a ballet dancer among and around players as he makes his play also beautiful to the eye, even for the losing side. A great winning play is most often also beautiful.

Why, you ask, should I be concerned about making my play beautiful? Simply because if you do, all the positive elements in play are able to flow through you. The result will not only be good but healthy and you will feel either like you don't want to stop or you are automatically "invited back." There will come to you like a sixth sense a new openness to all that you are in the moment and all you are moving toward in the eternal. Keats said, " 'Beauty is truth, truth beauty,' – that is all ye know on earth, and all ye need to know." And Jesus said, "Ye shall know the truth [the beautiful truth], and the truth shall set you free." What a difference it might make if we strove for symmetry rather than sweat, form over forensics, rhythm before rage, the comely over the cutthroat, winsome rather than winning, giving soul to body, and spirit to muscle.

If indeed the great playing experience between humans occurs when we make love, what better time to remember the beautiful with our words, hands, eyes, voice, mouth, and the lovely instruments God gave us to create the most beautiful thing we know – a child. If the greatest play is loving, and "beautiful" is the ultimate description for the most creative moment between humans, then we should try to make beauty a deep part of all play, and thus stay tuned for beautiful loving – sex with soul.

For the final letter, "Y," I could not ignore the riches of the Chinese *Yin-Yang*, the *Ta Ki*, and have also included for the eye not only the traditional symbol, but a superimposed image of a tree, giving us a great summary metaphor of play.

The circle is halved by a sigmoid line, creating a dynamic tension that a straight line would not. The light side signifies the masculine principle, Yang, and the dark side represents the feminine principle, Yin. In the Yin-Yang without the tree there is a dark dot in the white half and a light dot in the dark half, further developing the complex force-field generated by this powerful symbol, as each half participates more than symbolically in the other. Each principle is *resident in the other, neither yet both. We preserve these elements with The Cosmic Tree*, whose white roots penetrate deeply into the fecund underworld of the feminine, while the dark trunk and leaves rise triumphantly into the white heat of the masculine. Both male and female principles have their separate domain, while also including the necessary seed of the other.

The Yin is passive and represents the intuitional and feminine, the soft and supple, the earth and dark waters, trees and animals of the night, swamp creatures and flowers, the soul. The Yang is active, representing reason and the masculine, mountains, the sun and solar creatures, the high and hard, the dry places and the sky, birds of the day, dragons, unicorns and other fabulous inventions of play. Together, the Yin and Yang are a perfect balance of two great energies in the universe, and at the level of our own humanness they symbolize us, male and female also balanced and equal with each carrying the germ of the other, moving and alive in a marvelous dance, holding one another not in clinging dependency or wrestling anger, but with the joyous embrace of profound recognition and creative connection.

I regret that I do not know the artist who created *The Cos-*

mic Tree, but I use my daughter's version of it here with gratitude because I think it is much more than a frivolous
embellishment of the ancient Yin-Yang. While it is hard to
imagine adding anything to that perfect symbol, at least in this
context, I think the tree is helpful and not offensive. For me, the
tree brings a life to an abstract form that suggests the awe-
filled wonder of heaven and earth, sun and moon, man and
woman, and other marrying opposites. Rooted in the underwa-
ters of the feminine, it grows into the sunlight of the masculine,
and stands at the center of this earth garden connecting Great
Mother and Great Father. The tree is nearest kin among our
vegetative neighbors, breathing in for our good our deadly
breath as we breathe back its healing oxygen.

Thus, our play reaches the symbolic heights and depths of
our universe as we become first and every man and woman, re-
capitulating the moving away of opposites until we inevitably
meet in a life embrace that sweeps us into the great cosmic
dance, which we all share for such a wondrous moment. In that
moment of our lives we love one another, work together and play
the play of gods. We make the world a holier place with our loving, a healthier place with our working, and a happier place with
our play. We are born apart to bring all things together, to break
down the walls of separation, to find our essence in the other –
black in white and white in black; male in female and female in
male; feeding roots and the light-sipping leaves growing each
other; leaf-tree above and root-tree below, male and female
joined. What ecstatic play just to be alive in each other's eyes,
arms and ears, breathing and rooting for this breathless moment, in the eternal grafting of ourselves to all life behind us
and before – forever.

Chapter 8

CREATING THE FUTURE TOGETHER

"I just live from day to day," said the young wife. "My husband refuses to share any of his plans with me, if he has any. There is nothing to look forward to. The other day at his sister's house – she has a three-week-old little girl – he had the gall to say, 'Why don't we have another baby?' I just looked at him and laughed. That's as close as we ever get to planning. The two we have were accidents. Our whole life is just one accident after another."

Why Some Couples Do Not Plan Together

Many couples refuse to plan together. Understanding why we refuse is the first step toward changing the situation. We must consciously set goals and set strategies to bring those goals toward fruition. Following are a few reasons why couples refuse to plan. It may be helpful to see if any of these block your planning.

1. A Need to Control

One may need to maintain control of the marriage generally or of some specific aspect central to the relationship, such as sex or money. The mate's controlling influence then permeates the marriage to neutralize the other's input in important matters. The neglected spouse simply resigns from the process and, by default, power and control are retained by the other. *Questions:* Which of us holds the power in this marriage? Why? How is that power used to nurture and enhance our lives together to mold the future?

2. Reluctant Mate

One partner may be only "half in the marriage." To plan or dream together is to imply a commitment beyond where a spouse is or wants to be. Half-attentive responses, such as "Yeah, we'll have to talk about that sometime," often reflect the spouse's attitude, especially if the issue is important and clearly needs attention. Discussions that require long-term planning will be consistently avoided by the reluctant mate. *Questions:* Do we constantly shelve the big issues? Why?

3. Deprecation of the Mate

"You are terrible at planning or making decisions, so I have to do it." The mask for such arrogance in power is usually, "Look at the time you . . ." and some painful failure is cited. One man shyly attempted to begin his journey toward autonomy when he asked his mothering wife, "Well, I decided to marry you, didn't I?" He was immediately sabotaged with her retort, "No, dear, I decided that you would marry me if I asked you to." *Questions:* Is one of us made to feel put down as inadequate for the decisionmaking processes of our marriage? Which of us? Why?

4. Feelings of Inferiority

A wife says she wants her husband to make the decisions and do the planning because she does not trust her own judgment. In what matters? Under what circumstances? In discussion with whom? Some such women plan and decide quite well when the husband is absent. They do well with their own routine, with household concerns, in emergencies, or at work. Deference may have more to do with one's mate than with the real ability of the one opting out. For example, some men need dependent and weak wives in order to feel like men. If there are honest feelings of inferiority, these should be given attention rather than allowing them to cripple the planning process. *Questions:* Does one of us appear to be or feel inferior? What are *we* doing about such feelings?

5. Fear of Results

One may actually fear suggesting that the planning be shared. Humiliation, the "silent treatment," dumping ("Okay, if you're so smart, you do it"), or even physical abuse may counsel one to leave the subject alone. Or perhaps there is the fear that if the thing fails, one will blame the other. *Questions:* Do we cop out by blaming each other? What is the *real* issue here?

6. Refusal of Responsibility

One mate simply does not like taking responsibility. It is safer and more comfortable to follow. The exceptions among such persons are interesting. One may make little decisions and shun the big ones, even in the face of proof that the little ones are more important. *Questions:* Is it fair or healthy for our marriage if one of us exempts himself or herself from planning and deciding the course of the marriage out of some childish rejection of responsibility? Which of us does this?

7. Entrapment

This is especially annoying. A mate reneges on planning in order to "catch" the other in a mistake: "Well, it was your decision. I trusted you." I am amazed how some people continue to let their mates do this to them, even when they know the game. Occasionally it is a passive-aggressive way for one to "get" the other for a totally unconnected grievance. *Questions:* Do we ensnare or ambush each other with perverse "Bang! I-gotcha" delight in the other's well-intentioned failure? And is one of us now gun-shy?

8. Fear of Failure

This, of course, is probably the most universal reason for not planning. To think ahead, set goals, make plans, and take action only to have a failure is no fun. We resign ourselves to something called "fate," "God's will," or "The best-laid plans of mice and men . . . ," or "Something always happens anyway," and decide to drift in the name of absurdity, piety, spontaneity, or a raw, chin-into-the-wind courage that is sheer foolishness. Questions: Do we avoid planning by making poor excuses because we are terrified of failure? Do we cop out with a shoulder-shrugging acceptance of some sense of "what the hell" that robs us of our power.

9. Fear of Success

With a little sleight-of-hand, we can turn the "chicken" of the

previous fear back into the "egg" of this one, and so we are
caught in the chicken-or-the-egg syndrome. For some of us, to
succeed is to fail, and to fail is to succeed. Some people just
seem to proceed from one failure to the next. And others, as the
saying goes, snatch failure from the jaws of success. If we succeed, we may ruin our image of loser, become strangers in our
own world, have to continue being a winner, share it with our
relatives, quit being a martyr for which we feel rewarded, or re-
arrange our psychology of death since we can't take it with us —
some such nonsense that keeps us stuck on hold. This may well
be the worst fear of all. It is surely one of the most prevalent.
Ask yourself and your mate if either or both of you might be af-
flicted with this fear. Where does it come from in your life or
your family system? What is the payoff for such a psychology?
And what might happen if you gave it up? How can you break
the spell? When will you know for sure it is broken?

Preparing to Plan

1. Recalling and Sharing the Past: What Happened?
     We must embrace our past. We enrich each other with our
own personal history, apart and together. Old memories surface
again. Things buried are held up to the light for understanding.
We inform the marriage with our adult "show-and-tell." We tell
what hurt us and what felt good. Feelings are deepened, others
released. We hear and touch each other's past and are thus better able to understand the present and plan the future.
     Betty and John had been married two years after a short ac-
quaintance and engagement. They were now talking seriously
about having a baby. John saw that Betty could not really get
her feelings into the conversations. When confronted she said,
"You will be a great dad, but something is not ready yet. I
would like to know *us* better. Not that I expect to find something that will change my mind about having a baby. I want
that, but not yet. For example, I have never even met your
grandparents, your mother's folks. Perhaps we should just fly
out there and spend a few days with them. I have never talked
for more than five minutes alone with your father. Your mother
is like a stranger, except I think she likes me, and I know she en-
joys really nice clothes. Oh, it's not that bad. But you don't

know my folks either, not really. My parents knew each other's
families for three generations. Don't you have the feeling that
you would like to know more about where I'm coming from? I
don't mean before we *dare* have a baby. In some ways knowing
you better has absolutely *nothing* to do with having a baby, and
in other ways it has *everything* to do with it. Do you know what
I mean?"

Happily, John did. Some might say they should have done all
this before marriage. Perhaps so. They had not. So now they
took some time doing what John called a "little investigative re-
porting." They visited and talked, sharing impressions and feelings:

> Okay, tell me about little boys. You were one once. What's
> the real lowdown on those little guys? I've heard some
> strange things. (*Smiling*) If we ever have a boy, I want to
> be prepared.
> Will you please tell me why the subject was always changed
> when your Uncle Jeff was mentioned?
> My folks had a terrible fight one night. I cried myself to
> sleep. Next morning it was like nothing had happened. I
> was afraid to ask questions. I started worrying about us. I
> often had stomachaches. I'll never forget that night. Even
> now I don't like fights. They tear me up inside. I'll do any-
> thing not to rock the boat, and, as you say, that's not fair. I
> wilt on you sometimes.
> Remember the night after our first date when you called me
> real late and my father was furious? Well, how would you
> like for me to tell you why he was so angry?
> Since we got into this, I feel I have a whole library of short
> stories about us that begin "Let me tell you about the
> time." Sharing me and learning about you has been one of
> the most exciting things I've ever done.

2. Checking out the Present: What's Happening?

The past and future meet in the present. Since nothing new is
happening in the past and the future is still "on the way," we live
now, in the moment. We hold on to our history and welcome our
arriving life today, in the present. Our lives are lived in moments. If you miss the moment you lose your life.

Therefore, couples need to stay current with one another and regularly ask of themselves, What's happening to you, in you, around you, for you, and because of you? What is special about the life you are now living, and how do you see me sharing it with you?

We live like fish in a rich and teeming sea, and we are so much a part of the water that we cannot distinguish where sea ends and fish begins. Hence, we must be curious to sort out the tangled "now" of feelings and experiences by listening, reflecting, and interpreting together.

> I've been watching you, and you're not reading that book at all. Is something bothering you?
>
> What a party! Being your husband is a lot of fun!
>
> I thought I had gotten over the blowup at work yesterday, but driving in this morning, I had an overwhelming urge to just keep on going. I felt I never wanted to see that office and those people again. Do you mind just talking about it with me? I've got to flush some stuff.
>
> Please don't touch me that way. Here, put your hand under mine and follow me. There. See? That's better. Now, that's very nice. Very nice, indeed. Thank you. Now relax your mouth.
>
> Waiting for you here took me back to when we were first dating. It seems so long ago. Just nine years. Does it seem long to you?
>
> I know Jim's death was a terrible loss. Don't forget, I loved him too. But you just must not sit here and stare out the window, like you do so much. It has been almost two months since the funeral. Please talk to me.

Before we try to invent the future, we should attempt to get a clear fix on *now*. Once, while leading a "Friends, Partners, and Lovers" workshop, I asked the couples to fantasize responses to this question: If marriage is a house, what room are you in, and what's happening?

Following are a few of their answers. *Before you read them, do your own fantasy*: Close your eyes and picture yourself in or around the house. What is happening that might reflect where you are and what's happening in your marriage?

Front Door

I can't seem to get in. The door is locked. It's cold and raining. There are no lights on inside. I feel lonely and depressed.

Living Room

Our family is sitting in front of the fireplace popping popcorn and telling favorite stories. Everyone is happy and teasing.

I am a life-size poster hanging on the wall of the fireplace. All the furniture is gone. No one is there. I slowly peel off the wall like a window shade and fall to the floor. I couldn't watch any more.

I am old, sitting in a rocking chair by a window. My cat is in the sun on the sill. Outside children are playing in the street. A little girl is watching them. She looks like me at eight. I feel sad. You see, I am only thirty-two, but I feel very old and quite young at the same time. Where is the now me, the real me? Worst of all, both of my people are just watching, not doing much of anything themselves. Both of me are only observing life. That's actually true, you know. John complains that I never want to do anything.

Dining Room

Our meals are a kind of communion. We talk and sing at our table. The kids are small. We play guessing games after the meal. Nick does the dishes (Boy, that's a fantasy!) while the kids and I sit in a circle on the floor in the kitchen eating bowls of ice cream. (That seems silly.) Nick fusses. He has to talk around us and do the dishes while we just eat ice cream and laugh. Wow, I like that!

Bedroom

I am in bed with my wife. Sex is a big deal at our house. The kids are banging at the door. My wife and I are laughing so hard we can't do anything, or at least I can't.

My husband and I are in bed. This is where we most experience intimacy. He suddenly becomes a small boy, a baby, and then I am nursing him. Then he is himself again and we move to climax. The little boy, baby, parts bother me. He acts that way quite often. Even talks baby talk. I wish we could discuss that, but I am afraid I will hurt his feelings.

Bedtime with the children means stories, time to talk, songs, and prayers. We are all together – Tom, Eric, Rachel, and me – on Eric's bed this time. We are happy. I feel good. Simple as that.

I am asleep. That's all. In the fantasy I just watch me sleep. Since my husband's affair eight months ago, I am apt to sleep a lot, even though all that is over, and we have talked it all out. Should I be sleeping that much? Sometimes it scares me.

I am naked in front of my mirror. I am fat, maybe two hundred pounds. I actually weigh one thirty-six, although I "think fat" no matter what I weigh. My husband complains a lot. He says he knows when I gain even a couple of pounds. He's balding. Think I will tell him that.

Bathroom

I am sitting on the side of the tub, slumped over. The children are banging on the door. I am just sitting there crying. This is strange. I'd never do a thing like that to my children.

I am sitting in the tub with the shower going and the tub filling. I am at peace. I really dig hot water. I like to soak. My wife thinks all my bathing is not very masculine. She says I should go soak my head.

I am flushing the john over and over, but I can't seem to get everything to go down. It is like my marriage. Down the tube a little at a time, day after day. Six years flushed. I can't seem to take my hand off the handle.

Hall Closet

I hide in there like a little kid. I don't know what from. It's dark and I am scared. I hear my heart beating. A light starts going on and off. I see myself and then I can't. It's like strobing. I look different each time the light flashes. I get older. I open my eyes before I become a wrinkled old woman. I did not like this exercise. I do not recommend it for future workshops.

I am standing in the closet with the door closed, wearing my London Fog. Sherlock Holmes. I am spying on my wife. She comes in the house with my older brother. He opens the closet door and I strangle him. It is ghastly. I thought of opening my eyes, but had to see the end (ha!). My wife screamed and ran. Police came. I was arrested. My wife cried. When I got into the squad car, I looked back and saw her splitting her sides laughing. There is no truth in all this. I do not even have a brother. Could the "brother" be my mother's second husband? My real dad died. This guy looks real young for his age (forty-eight), and he gives my wife a lot of attention. This is stupid. Why did we do this fantasy thing?

Kitchen

I was cooking a fantastic meal. I like that room. I forget my problems there. I feel creative. Sometimes I even get the proverbial pat on the bottom by my wife. She did in the fantasy. I kissed her and left two big hand prints of flour on the back of her blue skirt, and she went out to work without knowing it. Fun fantasy. Like doing it. Think I'll try the hand part for real next time I cook bread and she's wearing a blue skirt. I think we have a real good marriage.

I am frying at the stove. It flames up. I run out the back door into my neighbor's arms. (He is here, so do not read this aloud if you plan to.) He whirls me around and laughs. I am screaming fire, fire. But he keeps laughing and whirling me around. Firemen arrive and squirt water all over both of us and we fall apart. I remember my brother throwing water over two copulating dogs in our yard when I was little. This is an awful fantasy, but I can really see what you are getting at. This is too personal, but I wanted to share it with you. What do you think might happen if I told my husband this fantasy? I think I would feel better if I did. But I won't. At least not now.

Roof

I am on the roof like Santa – costume, deer, the works. I look at my watch. It is seconds before midnight, like the Cinderella story, too. I reach in my bag. It is empty except for this one doll. I drop it down the chimney and sail away in my sleigh. (This is really strange.) I am here with my wife. Sue does not know it, but I have decided to file for divorce. My wife is pregnant. I don't know what it all means.

This fantasy has something to do with my decision, doesn't it?

Basement

Our rec room is transformed into a lovely ballroom with candles and everything, including a band. People are beautiful and dancing. I start down the stairs without any clothes on. My husband is at the bottom reaching out to me and smiling just as though I were dressed. I get halfway down and run crying back up the stairs. Everyone keeps dancing. My husband looks angry but does not follow me. I fall in a heap at the top sobbing. Then I see my husband dancing with a woman. It is me. I'm in both places. I don't understand, but I feel it is right for some reason. There is a truth about the fantasy. Me naked? H-mmm! You said we could interpret them. I fear my husband knowing me really well. I don't want the lights on when we make love even. But I love him and we enjoy each other. Am I getting close? I am glad I did this particular fantasy. It is clearer now. We should talk about my fears. I know very well what I am afraid of. It's a thing that happened. That's my story. You've had your fantasy.

A fantasy often mirrors the unconscious for us and can reveal impressions, ideas, and feelings about our lives. Without allowing ourselves to become bewitched or obsessed with the pictures of our fantasy, we may still be instructed. Those who use the "marriage as a house" fantasy frequently find that the fantasy provokes an important inquiry into the thinking, feeling, acting, and believing patterns of their marriage.

In the above fantasies, it became clear to each person that the unconscious was offering a little piece of drama which depicted feelings, attitudes, and conditions in their lives and marriages. Some of these were obvious and clear. Others were more obscure and symbolic. The man who saw his life-size poster peel off the wall was having an affair. He felt phony and not really a part of his family, even though he feigned loyalty and dabbled in family activities. The fantasy simply drove home his lack of integrity and commitment. He later entered therapy alone, then with his wife. The affair was dissolved, and the imperiled marriage received a new lease on life. All of this might have happened without the fantasy. Yet, he referred to the fantasy as "the flash of lightning" that woke him up to what he was doing.

Other fantasies were more like looking at the family album of happy scenes. This can be reassuring, unless one decides that the fantasy is high comedy, a farce, as evidenced by some tone or note of unreality. After a fantasy of a beautiful family experience, one man exclaimed, "But it is never really that way. Is the fantasy a longing I have or does it point to our pretention? Our family has to look good." He was a minister. Still other fantasies — there are many of these — are explicitly sexual. These are frequently insightful, raising to awareness the buried loneliness or longing. Some simply reflect the joy of intimacy in the life of the couple.

Fantasies are messengers. Sometimes it takes courage to answer the door when a messenger knocks. But, almost without exception, the knock is worthy of your answering it, and the message is enlightening. "What's happening" may best be revealed in fantasy when you stop to get in touch with your unconscious on stage. Couples who learn to share their fantasies are more apt to make connections where others fail and at greater depths. Fantasy is at least one additional way to picture the present.

3. Inventing the Future: What's Possible?

Two fundamental questions that lead us into adult life, and keep measuring our progress are the identity and destiny questions: "Who am I?" and "Where am I going?" We are already underway in this chapter with the destiny questions as they apply to marriage: Where are we going? Do we go out to meet the future or wait for it to arrive? If we go out, what is our disposition? Are we anxious about the treachery of fate? Are we hostile and brewing for vengeance? Or are we excited about the challenge and the possibility of reward? Do we reach out to tomorrow and expect to call it "good"?

Hey, Sally, I overheard Hal on the phone today talking with a lawyer about drawing up a will. He's only thirty-six. Why would he need a will? That's creepy. (*Pause*) Do you ever think about getting old? About dying?

Jim and Sarah have moved into their new house. It's beautiful. Suppose we will ever live like that?

The strangest thing just happened. You know Jeff's little new friend, Michael? Well, he just asked me why we go to church every Sunday. I told him it was because we enjoy it. But that doesn't sound right. Now I'm wondering why we do go. When I was a kid, I was afraid I would die and go to hell if I didn't. We need to talk about church some time. I have a feeling it is more tied up with what we're trying to get done with our lives than I thought.

The law degree? That was years ago. I've given up on that. You have any idea how long that takes, and how much money? Besides, I'm ten years older than the kids in law school today. You're a crazy man, but I love you. (*Pause*) Mom would love taking care of Phillip for me, wouldn't she? And you did get that neat raise last month. No, it's ridiculous.

I think I would add ten years to my life if we just lived on a piece of lakefront property.

As a team we invent our future. We dream the possibilities of our destiny together. We are not the masters of our fate, but we might be the architects drawing the blueprints and the artists lifting life off the paper and giving it soul. That is quite a lot toward creating our lives.

Exercises

Try one or more of the following:
1. Write letters to each other, with three paragraphs beginning as follows:
    a. "If you and I continue as we are, in five years I can see us . . ."
    b. "However, if we have enough love and courage, we will . . ."
    c. "All of which can lead us into the life that I dream of for us, namely . . ."
Swap letters; read them carefully and discuss each paragraph. Note similarities and differences in the way you are

seeing the future. Now what will you do about these fantasies? Find the action.
2. Divide a piece of writing paper into four equal parts. In each section write one of the four following headings:

One-Year Goals
Two-Year Goals
Five-Year Goals
Long-Range Goals

In each section list what you want to see accomplished by and for the two of you in each time frame. Be imaginative and willing to take risks. Now exchange papers and compare dreams.
3. Answer the following questions:
   a. What is your best talent/skill?
   b. Does that talent/skill need and deserve improvement?
   c. How might you better express that talent/skill?
   d. Is there a market for it that could bring greater satisfaction and/or money?
   e. Would you really like to make your talent/skill a more central part of your life? If so, how might you do this?
   f. Do you need a workable plan for organizing your life more effectively to deal with your talent/skill?
   g. If so, will you make a plan *now*? If not now, why not? When will you?
   h. How will you feel if you do nothing more than you are presently doing with your talent/skill?
   i. Is this talent/skill something that does or could enhance your marriage? If so, how?
   j. How does your mate feel about your talent/skill? How do other relatives and friends feel about it? (Support, tease, criticize?)
   k. If your plan works, what are the rewards? Sacrifices?
   l. So, if it works, will it all be worth the effort?
   m. How might success affect your marriage?
   n. If that first option does not work, where do you go from there to avoid getting caught in the win/lose syndrome we discussed earlier?
   o. Stop right here. What are you now feeling? Is it a *go, stop,* or *caution* feeling? Now exchange papers and discuss *feelings* carefully along with the answers and ideas. Ask:

What does my mate seem most to need from me right now?

4. Think of your body moving through time and space. What sort of traveler are you? What sort is your mate? How able are these two to travel together? Following are some suggestions, but don't let these limit you. Find your own.

jaunter	runner
jogger	walker
charger	stroller
tiptoer	slider
crawler	cartwheeler
racer	tumbler
hopscotcher	swinger (Tarzan/Jane)
creeper	floater
stumbler	strider

Is there something in the way you move together that will have a decisive impact on the way you create your future together? Think about your rhythms, frequencies, postures, cadences. Are you more often in or out of "sync" with one another? How does this affect the action field of your marriage, especially as you look toward the future?

5. Do an art fantasy. You need four pieces of paper at least 8 1/2 by 11 inches, plus finger paints or colored pens, something with which to put color on a page. Let your fantasy soar. Do four pictures in this order with the following themes:

Where am I now?

What is the force or power that prevents me from changing?

What would enable or facilitate my changing?

What will I look like when I arrive?

After you have completed the series, get your mate's remarks before you try to "explain" your work. See what she or he "sees" first. Are you saying something "new" about yourself? Are the forms flowing or tight and meticulous? How do the colors make you feel? Is there significant "movement" in the process from the first to the fourth piece?

6. Play Checkup. Do this acrostic game with FUTURE:

F = Facts   State how things are with you *now*.

U = Upset   Are you upset with the way things are?

	Check feelings: depression, anxiety, anticipation, urge to move on, anger, disappointment, etc. Just how upset are you, really?
T = Truth	Find the truth of what's possible. Now be honest with yourself. Shouldn't you play it safe and stay put? Who knows what's out there? What did you ever make happen by the sheer will of you? What is the truth of you as someone who makes things happen?
U = Ultimates	What are you after, finally? Complete the sentences: "Sooner or later I want . . ." "If I die without . . ." "Unless I get moving, . . ."
R = Resources	Name and measure on a scale of 1 to 10 your best resources, all of them that come to mind. What will it take to get to them and have them all working for you?
E = Enjoy	What pleasures can you anticipate from your dream? What permanent gain from the top options? What new discovery about you? What joy?

Swap your notes and see how the game informs you about the marriage. What do you have to share with one another? How do your dreams match? Where might you compromise? Can both achieve?

7. Fantasize together future trouble spots:
   a. A child "goofs up" or has a special need.
   b. Death or incapacity of a parent.
   c. Your retirement.
   d. Financial stress.
   e. Let your mind "float" through your family world and see where trouble spots and challenges stop you. Pay attention to these, no matter how farfetched your fantasy may seem. Discuss them.

There is a great story coming out of the construction of the Frank Lloyd Wright house in Fallingwater, Pa. Word has it that when the day came to take down the beams that supported the enormous, cantilevered patios of great slabs of steel-reinforced concrete, the workmen refused because of the danger. Both the foreman and contractor failed to move the men to do the job. Finally, the architect himself arrived to persuade the workers. With a speech and blueprints he spoke of his knowledge of physics, stress factors, and the materials used. Their response said something like, "Yeah. Sure. But that down there is paper, and that up there is concrete." Finally, in exasperation, Wright grabbed a sledgehammer and began stalking up and down the rows of posts, smashing the supports, and breaking open the future with his bare hands as the workmen fled. Over him hung tons of concrete, as he bet his life on his dream. Today the building stands as a monument to the man and an important milepost in an evolving American architecture.

In a life worth living we are often betting our lives on our dreams. In marriage one mate may often seem like Frank Lloyd Wright risking great danger, perhaps destruction, while the other one trembles a bit at the audacity. Will it work? Are we crazy? Can we survive? In marriage it is best if both are building the dream, and both are tearing out the superfluous supports, partners in it all. Friends fantasize the future with an inventive humor. Lovers embrace their dream with a sense of mystery *and* fillment. Partners roll up their sleeves and get to work. It takes all three – friend, partner, lover – to make this union bring forth, again and again. Stretch, reach, and claim what is yours together.

SELECTED BIBLIOGRAPHY

Allen, Gina, and Martin, Clement G. *Intimacy*. New York: Pocket Books, 1972.

Arieti, Silvano. *Creativity, the Magic Synthesis*. New York: Basic Books, 1976.

Bassein, Beth Ann. *Women and Death*. Westport, Conn.: Greenwood Press, 1984.

Berne, Eric. *What Do You Say After You Say Hello?* New York: Grove Press, 1972.

Buber, Martin. *I and Thou*, trans. Walter Kaufman. New York: Charles Scribner's Sons, 1970.

Campbell, Joseph, ed. *The Portable Jung*. New York: Viking Press,1971.

Comfort, Alex. *The Joy of Sex*. New York: Crown Publishers, 1972.

———. *More Joy of Sex*. New York: Crown Publishers, 1975.

deCastillejo, Irene C. *Knowing Woman*. New York: Harper & Row, 1973.

Frankl, Viktor E. *Man's Search for Meaning*, rev. ed. Boston: Beacon Press, 1963.

Fromm, Erich. *The Art of Loving*. New York: Harper & Row, 1956.

Gadon, Elinor W. *The Once and Future Goddess*. San Francisco: Harper, 1989.

Gonzalez-Cruise, F. *On the Nature of Things Erotic*. New York: Harcourt Brace Jovanovich, 1988.

Hamacheck, Don E. *Encounters with Self*. New York: Holt, Rinehart and Winston, 1971.

Hillman, James. *Insearch: Psychology and Religion*. New York: Charles Scribner's Sons, 1967.

Hite, Shere. *The Hite Report*. New York: Dell, 1977.

Johnson, Robert A. *Ecstasy: Understanding the Psychology of Joy*. San Francisco: Harper & Row, 1989.

———. *Femininity Lost and Regained*. New York: Harper & Row, 1990.

———. *He!* King of Prussia, Pa.: Religious Publishing Company, 1974.

———. *She!* King of Prussia, Pa.: Religious Publishing Company, 1976.

———. *We: Understanding the Psychology of Romantic Love*. San Francisco: Harper & Row, 1989.

Jung, Carl. *Memories, Dreams and Reflections*. New York: Vintage Books, 1961.

Keen, Sam. *To a Dancing God*. New York: Harper & Row, 1970.

———. *The Passionate Life: Stages of Loving*. San Francisco: Harper, 1983.

———. *Fire in the Belly: On Being a Man*. New York: Bantam Books, 1991.

Lowen, Alexander. *Pleasure*. New York: Penguin Books, 1975.

Mace, David, and Mace, Vera. *We Can Have Better Marriages If We Really Want Them*. Nashville, Tenn.: Abingdon Press, 1974.

———. *How to Have a Happy Marriage*. Nashville, Tenn.: Abingdon Press, 1977.

Maslow, Abraham H. *Religions, Values and Peak Experiences*. Columbus, Ohio: Ohio State University Press, 1964.

Masters, William H., et al. *The Pleasure Bond: A New Look at Sexuality and Commitment*. Boston: Little, Brown, 1975.

May, Rollo. *Love and Will*. New York: W. W. Norton, 1969.

———. *The Courage to Create*. New York: W. W. Norton, 1975.

Michie, Helena. *The Flesh Made Word*. New York: Oxford Press, 1987.

Miles, Margaret R. *Carnal Knowing*. New York: Vintage Books, 1991.

Molton, Warren Lane. *Bruised Reeds*. Valley Forge, Pa.: Judson Press, 1970.

———. *Spheres of Intimacy*. Kansas City: Pinon Press, 1982.

Moore, R., and Gilliette, D. *King, Warrior, Magician, Lover*. New York: Harper, 1990.

Neale, Robert E. *In Praise of Play*. New York: Harper & Row, 1969.

Pederson, Loren E. *Dark Hearts: The Unconscious Forces That Shape Men's Lives*. Boston: Shambhala, 1991.

Pomeroy, Sarah B. *Goddesses, Whores, Wives and Slaves*. New York: Schocken Books, 1975.

Riesman, David. *The Lonely Crowd*. New Haven: Yale University Press, 1961.

Rogers, Carl. *On Becoming a Person*. Boston: Houghton Mifflin, 1961.

———. *Becoming Partners: Marriage and Its Alternatives*. New York: Delacorte Press, 1972.

Satir, Virginia. *Conjoint Family Therapy*. Palo Alto, Calif.: Science and Behavior Books, 1964.

———. *Peoplemaking*. Palo Alto, Calif.: Science and Behavior Books, 1972.

Singer, Jerome L. *The Inner World of Daydreaming*. New York: Harper & Row, 1975.

Singer, June. *Androgyny*. New York: Doubleday, 1976.

Steiner, Claude. *Scripts People Live*. New York: Grove Press, 1974.

Stevens, John O. *Awareness: Exploring, Experimenting, Experiencing*. Lafayette, Calif.: Real People Press, 1971.

Storr, Anthony. *Solitude: A Return to the Self*. New York: Free Press, 1988.

Additional Resources Published by Judson Press

By Myself But Not Alone: A Prayer Journal for Divorced Moms, Barbara Owen. 0-8170-1201-X

Child Sexual Abuse: A Handbook for Clergy and Church Members, Lee W. Carlson, 0-8170-1133-1

Christian Parenting, Lee W. Carlson, ed. 0-8170-1072-6

Church Family Gatherings, Joe Leonard, Jr., ed. 0-8170-0809-8

Church in the Life of the Black Family, The, Wallace C. Smith. 0-8170-1040-8

Devotions for New Mothers, Bonnie Taylor. 0-8170-1115-3

For Any Young Mother Who Lives in a Shoe, Mary Tobey Marsh. 0-8170-1170-6

Poems of a Son, Prayers of a Father, Matthew L. Watley, William D. Watley. 0-8170-1183-8

Premarital Counseling Handbook for Ministers, Theodore K. Pitt. 0-8170-1071-8

Springtime of Love and Marriage, The, James R. Hine. 0-8170-1064-5

Willing to Try Again: Steps Toward Blending a Family, Dick Dunn. 0-8170-1185-4